D0726386

Finance for the Non-financial Manager

CITY MANAGEMENT COURSES

Also available in this series
THE 12-DAY MARKETING PLAN
THE SHORTER MBA

Finance for the Non-financial Manager

All you need to know about business finance

John Harrison

Thorsons
An Imprint of HarperCollins*Publishers*

Thorsons
An Imprint of HarperCollins*Publishers*
77–85 Fulham Palace Road,
Hammersmith, London W6 8JB

Published by Thorsons 1989
7 9 10 8 6

A catalogue record for this book
is available from the British Library

ISBN 0 7225 1901 X

Printed and bound in Great Britain by
Woolnough Bookbinding, Irthlingborough, Northamptonshire

Contents

Introduction

Accountancy is called 'the language of business'. This is because measures of success and failure in business are expressed in financial terms. As a result, people who have a working knowledge of this language are far better placed to take an active role in key business decisions.

Knowledge of the basics of accountancy is especially useful for those running small businesses. Small businesses are particularly vulnerable to failure when those making decisions cannot appreciate the current financial status of the business or do not understand the financial implications of their intended actions. It is also important that people in management and supervisory roles in larger businesses have this knowledge as well. As individuals develop their careers, they tend to become more and more involved in financial matters. This might happen because, for example, they take on budget responsibilities, become involved in the appraisal of investment opportunities, or take on project management in any of the numerous other areas of business which have financial implications.

At one time, such knowledge was mainly required in the commercial business sector, but nowadays, public sector organizations tend to be run along commercial lines. The simple fact is that virtually everybody who has management or supervisory responsibility can benefit from having a reasonable level of financial awareness. Furthermore, possession of such awareness can, in some cases, make a significant contribution to prospects of promotion into more senior positions, where a broader commercial view is often required.

The purpose of this book is to provide a basic understanding of finance for the non-accountant. Fortunately, as all business finance is based on common structures, concepts and disciplines, the same basics of finance apply in a small new business venture as in a well-established multinational corporation. This means that the information provided in this book applies equally as well to the small independent businessman as to the supervisor or manager in a larger organization.

Of course, as businesses grow, the volume and complexity of the financial transactions made increase. Furthermore, the use of computers allows for much more sophisticated methods of recording, processing and presenting financial data. Nevertheless, it is important to remember that the same basic procedures underpin all accounting systems, computerized or not. This means that the knowledge you gain from this book can be applied in *any* business situation, although some interpretation may be necessary in specific circumstances.

The scope of the book

First of all, it is important to note that this book is *not* designed to train the reader to become an accountant. Accountancy, like all professions, is a job which requires many years of training to perform properly. What it *is* designed to do is enable the reader to converse with, use and question accountants and the information they produce in an informed and intelligent way.

The book aims to provide:

- understanding of the language, terminology and structure of accounts — to enable better communication with accountants and analysts
- familiarity with the structure, content and purpose of the main financial statements:
  - ★ the profit and loss account
  - ★ the balance sheet
  - ★ the funds flow statement
- knowledge of the key factors which contribute to greater efficiency and increased profitability in the main areas of business — production, distribution, sales and administration
- an understanding of the importance of managing company assets — stocks, debtors, machinery etc. — and the measures and techniques used in controlling them.
- the ability to plan, evaluate and control budgeted and projected expenditure
- the skill to read, appreciate and review the contents of the annual report produced by a company.

The book contains practical exercises to aid understanding of some of these concepts. These are an integral part of the study process, and if you want to understand the topics discussed in the book thoroughly you should work through all the exercises carefully before checking your answers against the solutions provided at the back of the book. Readers may also find it useful to examine relevant examples of actual practice as carried out in their own organizations.

To make the best use of this book you should think of it as a training manual. It will be most helpful to you if you work through it from beginning to end in its logical sequence as some of the later chapters depend on explanations given in the earlier part of the book. Later you can use it as a work of reference, and dip into it to remind yourself of some of the techniques. To help with this, it is divided up into a large number of quite short chapters, each covering a different financial topic, and each introduced with a sentence explaining what that chapter covers.

Part 1 Financing the business

CHAPTER 1

The purpose of accounting

This chapter explains the purpose of accounting, and distinguishes between the terms *profit*, *cash* and *wealth*.

1.1 Defining 'finance' and 'accounts'

Let us start the chapter by defining what we mean by *finance* and *accounts*. *Finance* can mean either the *management* of money, as in the 'finance department', or a *source* of money, as in 'financing' a car purchase. By and large, we will be using the former definition in this book.

The term *accounts* is often used interchangeably with the term *finance* — the finance department of a company, for example, is often referred to as the 'accounts department'. But, strictly speaking, the term accounts refers to the *books of account* which form the basic accounting records of a business.

1.2 Profit, assets and wealth

Annual income: twenty pounds; annual expenditure: nineteen nineteen six; result: happiness. Annual income: twenty pounds; annual expenditure: twenty pounds ought and sixpence; result: misery.

(Mr Micawber in *David Copperfield*, Charles Dickens.)

Over a hundred years ago, Mr Micawber was demonstrating the principle of simple personal accounts. Furthermore, this type of personal accounts calculation is likely to be familiar to us today — the management of personal finance! Most of us are concerned to manage our affairs so that our normal expenditure is covered by our wages or salary. In other words, over a period of time — a week, month or year — we would like to generate a surplus of income over expenditure — make a profit.

Unfortunately, life is made more complicated by the fact that, as well as income and expenditure, we may have some *assets* — possessions of value — or some other form of *wealth*.

We can illustrate this using the example of two colleagues, Fred and Joe. These two work together and have identical income and their spending pattern is almost identical. The one major difference between them is that Fred rents a council flat, whereas Joe is buying a house. Their income and expenditure each month is as follows:

Monthly transactions

	Fred £	Joe £
Income		
Take-home pay	500	500
Expenditure		
Property costs (including rates, services etc.)	150	200
Other expenditure (food, clothes, car etc.)	300	300
Monthly surplus	50	—

As things stand in the average year, Fred generates a surplus of 12×£50=£600, which he puts into his building society account. Joe on the other hand, saves nothing. Who do you think is better off?

*Write your answer here*______________________________________

Well, it certainly *looks* as though Fred is the wealthier, but let us look a little closer. If we inspect their relative cash positions as they exist at the moment, we discover the following:

Current cash positions

	Fred £	Joe £
Accumulated savings	5,000	—

Although they are lodged in the building society, Fred's savings can be classified as cash as they are easily convertible. So, who is better off on a cash basis?

Again, write your answer down ______________________________________

Once more, Fred appears to be in the better position. Finally, let us judge them by the assets they own (ignoring the contents of their properties — televisions, furniture and so on — which are roughly comparable).

Assets owned at the present time

	Fred £		Joe £
Second-hand car	1,000		1,000
Cash (in building society)	5,000		–
Property value	–	30,000	
Less: amount owing on mortgage	–	(10,000)	
			20,000
Total assets	6,000		21,000

Now which one do we consider to be the better off?

Write down the name of the person who appears to be the wealthier?

From this example you can see that there are several different ways of measuring finance. Fred, for example, has a greater annual surplus than Joe, and much better cash resources. Joe, on the other hand, could be called the wealthiest, because, given time, he could realize much greater value than Fred.

1.3 The purpose of accounting

Let us now return to the title of this chapter — *the purpose of accounting* — and see what we can conclude from the simple accounts we have drawn up for Fred and Joe.

- In order to produce the figures at all, it is necessary to keep *records* of all the relevant financial transactions.
- The transactions are summarized to give *financial reports*. These either show the results over a period of time — the amount saved — or the situation at a point in time — the value of a house at a particular date.

A definition of the purpose of accounting might be therefore:

To provide records of all financial transactions, so that the financial position of a business and its relationship with the owners and interested outside parties can be determined.

The latter part of the definition refers to the funding of the business, together with the position on money owed *to* and *by* the business.

Although the simple financial records we created in the Fred and Joe example referred to individuals, the principles used apply to *any* financial undertaking.

In accounting, the three most important financial reports, or summaries of accounts, are:

- The surplus (or deficit), which can be expressed as profit (or loss), generated during a period of time.
- A statement on the cash position. This is sometimes known as the liquidity position.
- The wealth or value of assets of the organization at a point in time.

This applies whether the 'organization' is an individual, a partnership, a company, or an international corporation. So, although a business may have made many more transactions than an individual, the accounts will be put together using the same principles. The simple surplus, cash and wealth statements developed above will be seen again and again throughout this book.

CHAPTER 2

The aims of business

This chapter shows how accounts need to reflect the aims and objectives of business. It also reviews the main users of financial reports and defines wealth and profit.

2.1 What are we in business for?

If accounts are to be used for measuring company performance, it is necessary to understand the aims and objectives of business. Only then can the contents of the accounts be made to act as the 'language of business' and report performance against our pre-set targets. At this point, it would be easy to be cynical and adopt the popular view that the purpose of business is simply to create the greatest possible profit for the owners. Certainly, *one* of the objectives of a company should be to make profits. However, this should not be the *only* objective. The reason for this is that there are a number of other factors that have long been recognized as contributing to the maintenance of continuous and sound company growth over a period of time. These factors are shown in the *virtuous circle*, demonstrated by the diagram below.

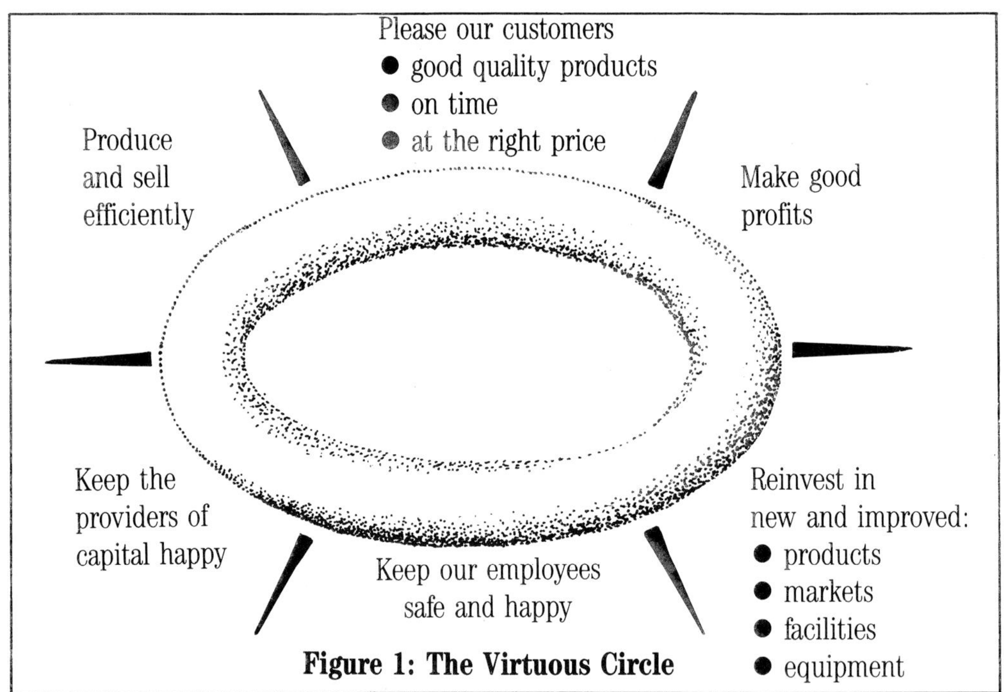

Figure 1: The Virtuous Circle

Failure in any one of the elements of the circle can jeopardize the natural growth and increased wealth that should occur each time we go around the circle. The aim of a company should therefore be to satisfy *all* the major criteria upon which success depends.

The Accounting Standards Steering Committee, the management group representing the accountancy profession, questioned the top 300 companies in the UK in order to discover what their objectives were. The results of the survey were published in a booklet called *The Corporate Report*. The booklet included the following statement of company purpose which incorporated broadly the full spectrum of objectives observed.

Our purpose in business

Our purpose in business is to create wealth, to make money. For this to be possible, we must please our customers and enjoy the confidence of our shareholders and employees. We must make good profits, so that, after providing for taxes and dividends (and, in present circumstances, financing inflation), there is enough money available to keep our factories and equipment modern and enable us to grow in strength and maintain or improve our market position. We endeavour to provide good, satisfying employment for our people. Creating wealth and building a better company is our contribution to better standards of living.

The Corporate Report

As you can see, this company statement is consistent with the virtuous circle.

2.2 The users of financial statements

Having defined the objectives of your business, you must not only design financial reports so that they measure the company's performance against each agreed objective, but also make the reports available to each interested party.

It is obvious that it is difficult, even impossible, to measure *all* of the objectives in purely financial terms. For example, how do you measure the quality of the staff employed by the company? For this reason, the annual report and accounts document, the major report on performance published by companies each year, includes narrative as well as financial results.

As we shall see later, the annual report and accounts statement has to satisfy the information requirements of the following interested groups:

- *The equity investor group* — the shareholders or owners
- *The loan creditor group* — banks and other lenders of money to the company
- *Employees and their representatives* — interested in continuous and profitable employment
- *Company management* — information to be used in controlling and managing the business
- *Analysts and advisors* — who advise potential shareholders and lenders of funds, or assess credit worth, etc.
- *The business contact group* — customers, suppliers, agents, distributors etc.
- *The government, national and local* — taxation, employment etc.
- *The general public* — in particular, consumers, the local community, etc.

The information requirements of these groups vary widely. Nevertheless, it is the *financial* performance of the company that determines the continuing existence of the business, and which is the top priority for most groups.

2.3 Wealth and profit

Before going any further, we must define *wealth* and *profit*, as these terms appear often throughout the text.

For an accountant, *wealth* represents the possessions or *assets* of a company or individual. In order to increase wealth, the company or individual must own more assets at the end of a period of time than they did at the start. The amount of wealth created in a period is called *retained profit*. Profit, therefore, represents *both*:

- the sum remaining from trading and investment after all debts have been paid. That is, after trading expenses, interest payable, taxation, dividends to investors and all other costs have been paid,

and

- the difference between wealth at the start of a period and wealth at the end.

Obviously, if a company is trading unsuccessfully or inefficiently, and thus not meeting its objectives, it may end up with less wealth at the end of the period than it started out with. If this happens, the company has made a *loss* in that period.

Exercise 1

List five major factors that help create wealth in a company:

(a) ____________________

(b) ____________________

(c) ____________________

(d) ____________________

(e) ____________________

The answers to all the exercises are at the back of the book.

CHAPTER 3

The mechanics of accounting

This chapter explains *double-entry bookkeeping* and defines *debits* and *credits*.

3.1 How do accounting records operate?

The earlier definition of the purpose of accounting quoted the recording of financial transactions as a key activity. We now need to discover how this is done.

The basic transaction-recording process — *bookkeeping method* — we use today has been developed over centuries. It is most easily explained by following this development. Public and private bookkeeping first began in ancient Egyptian, Greek and Roman times. In the public sector, the development of community organizations in these civilizations was accompanied by the need for appointed officials to account for their use of public funds. In other words, they were obliged to keep records of, and account for, income and expenditure, and to have these records checked (*audited*) by other officials.

On the other hand, in the private sector merchants and landowners would ask their agents to present an account of activities relating to the business or property. It became the custom for the owners to hire professional examiners of accounts — auditors — to check the accounts. These accounts were often presented verbally, and the term 'auditor' comes from the Latin *audire*, to hear.

These accounts were merely lists of income and expenditure, the sort of simple accounts that are still used for small organizations, such as clubs, today. However, by the fifteenth century, the larger Italian merchants had outgrown this system. Much of their wealth was tied up in stocks of merchandise, so they needed a system that could cope with valuations of assets and wealth as well as simple records of purchases and sales. A system was developed that could not only deal with different types of business transactions, but was also self-checking — the *double-entry system*. This system, first described by Pacioli in 1494, would you believe, still forms the basis of bookkeeping and accounts as we know them today.

Since then the major change in business has been the increasing complexity of ownership — from single merchants through joint ventures to today's multinationals with many thousands of shareholders. The double-entry system has been robust enough to cope with these changes, despite the demands for greater accountability as owners have become more remote from the day-to-day running of many commercial operations.

3.2 Double-entry bookkeeping

So, what distinguishes double-entry bookkeeping from other systems? Well, as the name suggests, each transaction is recorded twice — as a debit *and* as a credit. You may be familiar with these terms — a *debit* is money spent or owed to us, and a *credit* is income, or money owed by us to others.

The advantage of each entry being made twice is that, at the end of a given period of time, the value of credits should equal the total of debits. This is a basic test of accuracy. The statement of total debits and credits is known as a *trial balance.*

Before leaving this topic, let us see how each transaction is entered twice in basic books, by using as an example a few transactions that might take place at the commencement of a small business. By the way, it is useful to know that the basic books of account are divided into *ledgers* — sales ledger, purchases ledger — the name derives from the days when separate books were kept for each type of transaction. Nowadays, the entries are more likely to be input to a computer. However, the ledger structure is maintained within the computerized system.

In our example, the entries for the first period are as follows:

(1) £10,000 invested by the owner
(2) Workshop rented during period — £1,000
(3) Materials purchased and used — £2,000
(4) Wages paid — £2,000
(5) Cash sales — £6,000

The double-entry treatment would be as follows:

	Debit £	*Credit* £
(1) Debit cash book — cash invested	10,000	
Credit owner's capital account		10,000
(2) Rent (Profit and loss account)	1,000	
Cash book (payment)		1,000
(3) Materials (P&L account)	2,000	
Cash book (payment)		2,000
(4) Wages (P&L account)	2,000	
Cash book (payment)		2,000
(5) Sales income (P&L account)		6,000
Cash book (receipt)	6,000	

At this stage, we merely wish to demonstrate that each transaction is matched by an equal and opposite entry, and that total debits must equal total credits. Later on, when we deal with the financial reports, it is important to remember that each line of the report represents hundreds or even thousands of individual double-entry records like these.

Exercise 2

We saw in the text that a *debit* is money owing to us or a payment made, and a *credit* is money we owe, or income. Mark each of the following transactions as either a debit (D) or a credit (C). Ignore the equal and opposite entry.

(a) An electricity bill due for payment.

(b) An invoice outstanding for sales made.

(c) A bank overdraft.

(d) Components purchased.

(e) A factory purchased.

(f) VAT owed to HM Customs and Excise.

(g) Cash sales made.

By now you should be aware of the basic terminology of bookkeeping, so we will move on to review how companies are financed, and what they do with the finance they receive.

CHAPTER 3

Financing the business

This chapter describes the *sources of funds* used in setting up a business.

4.1 Where does the finance come from?

It is necessary to have funds (known as *capital*) in order to start a new business. This is because the business will need to provide for initial expenditure, such as renting or purchasing premises, paying for raw materials and wages, and so on.

A person starting up a business may have enough money to provide all the capital, but, more often, additional funds are required from other sources. Of course, even if a person *does* have the money, he or she may not want to risk it all in the business, and will therefore seek to fund all or part of the capital elsewhere. So, where does the money to finance a business come from?

The answer is that it flows in from three places:

- from the owners
- from bank loans or similar lenders
- once the business is established, from profits retained in the business.

In fact, it is similar to the way we would fund a personal project. When replacing a car, for example, we usually have three potential sources of finance:

- from our own savings
- from bank loans or other types of credit — from hire purchase companies for example
- from money retained from the sale of the old car.

Let us now look at the sources of business finance in more detail.

4.2 Share capital or owner's equity

Most businesses these days are set up as limited companies (Ltd) or as public limited companies (PLC). The owners of these businesses are the *shareholders*. The word 'Limited' means that the owners of the company are only liable for the debts of the company *up to the value of their share investment*. In other words, the most a shareholder can lose, if a venture or business fails, is the share capital he has invested in the business. This is not the case for businesses set up as partnerships, in which the partners are personally liable for the debts run up by the business. For this reason, partnerships are mostly restricted to professional occupations, such as doctors and solicitors, which have a low level of business risk.

People can invest in business by buying shares in a company thus becoming shareholders. Investors with more than a certain percentage of the shares in a company often have a say in the running of the organization. The total value of capital provided by shareholders in a company is known as the *share capital* or *owner's equity*.

In a small private company, the share

capital may only be £100 with shares owned by two or three people. By comparison, Lucas Industries PLC, a typical large company, has about 95 million shares issued owned by 18,000 individuals and companies.

4.3 Loan capital or long-term liabilities

A company may require funding in addition to share capital. If the owners do not wish to issue further shares and divide the ownership further they can arrange commercial loans. These loans may be from banks, from mortgages on properties, or debentures (a commercial loan similar to a mortgage).

Because they have no say in the running of the business, the providers of the loan will normally require some kind of guarantee. In a new company, the owners may be required to provide a personal guarantee (which in fact extends their liability beyond that of their share investment). In a mature company, the loans are normally given against the security of company assets. These so-called *charges on assets* give the lender priority in terms of recovering his loan should the business fail.

4.4 Reserves

Once a company is established, the funding of continued growth will mostly be derived internally, that is, out of retained profits. Once the trading profit is produced and any tax and interest paid, the remaining profit belongs to the shareholders. This remaining profit may be either paid out to shareholders as *dividends* — their equivalent to interest — or kept in the business to fund future growth. Usually, some is paid out and some retained. The amount retained is known as a *revenue reserve* if voluntarily retained, or a *capital reserve* if it arises because of a legal restriction on the amount paid out. The amounts retained as reserves remain part of the shareholders' equity, i.e., they are still the property of the shareholders.

The term *reserves* is one of the most misunderstood terms in accounting as it is often assumed that reserves are effectively a cash sum held available for emergencies. However, it is usually the case that the reserves have been or will be reinvested in the assets of the business, and do not, therefore, exist as cash.

Using a personal finance comparison, an individual may have saved £2,000 — made a 'profit'. This amount could be held as a cash reserve in a building society or bank account, or it could be invested in assets such as house insulation and double glazing. In the latter case the reserve will be represented by value rather than cash. In other words, the individual will be 'owed' £2,000 by his home as an improved asset.

CHAPTER 5

What is finance used for?

This chapter shows what the capital of a company is used for.

Having financed our company, we must now see what the finance is used for. Usually the funds are used in three ways:

- to purchase fixed assets
- to be used as working capital
- for investment.

We will look at these in more detail.

You might like to note that, although public organizations are funded differently (by public funds and sometimes by loans) their funds are used in a similar way to businesses.

5.1 Fixed assets

Fixed assets are purchased and owned by the business. They represent the means by which the company earns its profits. The term *fixed* is used, because they are not for sale in the normal course of business. They include such items as land, buildings, plant and machinery, office equipment, motor vehicles and computers. These are called the *tangible* fixed assets of the company because they can be seen and touched. Another type of fixed asset arises called *intangible* fixed assets. The most common intangible fixed asset is *goodwill*. This often arises, for example, when a business is purchased. In addition to the tangible assets purchased, a further sum may be paid out for the goodwill generated by the previous owner. In other words, a value is put on the efforts of the previous owner to build up trade and encourage custom, which obviously has a value to the new owner.

Expenditure on fixed assets is known as *capital expenditure*.

5.2 Current assets or working capital

The second use of company finance is to provide funds for the everyday operation of the business in terms of:

- raw materials, components and packaging for the production process
- goods and services purchased to maintain the fixed assets and allow the process to run
- labour to operate the processes and run the business.

In order to operate a company efficiently and effectively, some of the finance will also be spent on making the operations and processes of the business better. For example, we may wish to invest in bulk purchases of raw materials to obtain discounts, and hold reasonable raw material stocks to ensure smooth production. Other finance will be used to provide stocks of finished goods, so that immediate deliveries can be made to customers. We will also need to fund credit sales when it is the custom to do so.

If we stop our company at any moment

in time, we are likely to have working capital invested in:

- *Stocks*
  - ★ Raw materials and components
  - ★ Work in progress (WIP) particularly with long processes such as with aerospace projects
  - ★ Finished goods
- *Trade debtors*
  - ★ Money owed by customers
- *Bank and cash*
  - ★ Any surplus funds.

The more money we have tied up in these areas the less we have available to invest in growth of fixed assets. It is important therefore to keep stocks and debtors as low as possible — a subject we will be returning to later.

At the same time as discussing current assets, it is convenient to consider *current liabilities*. This is because, in the course of everyday operations, we not only invest funds as shown above, but we also create *liabilities* — sums of money that we owe. For example, if we buy goods and services on credit we owe our suppliers or *trade creditors*. Other creditors may include sums owed to the taxman and the shareholders. When we stop our company at a moment in time, the total of current liabilities, as money owing, is deducted from the current assets held at that time, to give *net current assets*.

Current assets – *Current liabilities*
= *Net current assets*

Current liabilities represent a reduction in the need for working capital.

5.3 Investments

Once a company is established, it may be in a position where it cannot profitably invest more money within the business as it stands. The directors of the business will then look outside the business to invest funds generated within the business.

If the money surplus is likely to be short term (that is, the money will be required by the business again in the near future) short-term investments will be made which can be easily reconverted back to cash as the need arises. If the surplus is continuing and long term, the directors will want to invest for the long term to get the most profitable return on investment. Investments considered might include:

- buying shares in other companies
- purchasing other companies outright
- making long-term loans
- investing in government stocks.

Many successful companies have tried to use their investments to diversify into other business areas. Some, for example the tobacco companies, do so because their current area of activity is shrinking. Others invest purely for growth reasons. There have been some interesting cases of companies that have bought into businesses that appeared attractive, but which proved to be extremely difficult to understand and manage. In the USA, for example, Warner Brothers, the film company, bought Atari, the computer and TV games operation. Shortly after the takeover, Atari made a loss of over $400 million in one quarter alone.

It is an interesting thought that one of the major 'assets' of a company is its workforce — a loyal and well-motivated workforce being far more likely to create wealth than a discontented one with a high turnover rate. Although the contribution of staff is often recognized, Marks and Spencer being an example of such a company, no *financial* asset value is put on staff. Professional football clubs are an exception to this — transfer fees show the value of their team members — although even these are not shown as assets.

Exercise 3

List the three main sources of company finance, and the three main uses to which the funds are put.

Sources *Uses*

____

____

____

____

____

____

CHAPTER 6

The financial reports Part 1

This chapter outlines the main financial reports included in the annual report and accounts of a business. The balance sheet is then explained in more detail.

Now we know the ways in which money flows into and out of a business, we can look at how these flows are reported.

The principal documents produced — the main financial records — are the *Profit and loss account* and the *Balance sheet*. These are terms with which most people in business are familiar, but they are also terms which most people would find hard to define. Furthermore, contrary to popular belief, many financial experts would rate the balance sheet as the more important document, with the profit and loss account merely adding information to supplement that provided by the balance sheet. Other major financial statements are the *Source and application of funds statement* (otherwise known as the *Funds flow statement*), and the *Statement of value added*.

It is important to understand the role of the major financial statements at this stage because not only are they the major internal financial reports, but they are also the key financial statements in the *Annual report and accounts*.

Each company has a legal obligation to produce an annual report. This report must be audited, and then presented to the shareholders at an annual general meeting. Finally, the report must be lodged with the Registrar of Companies at Companies House, where it is made available to the general public.

6.1 The balance sheet

A balance sheet is a picture of a company taken at a particular moment in time — a kind of freeze-frame. Moreover, it is a measurement of the wealth of a company at that moment, so when it is compared with an earlier balance sheet, it shows the growth of the company's wealth in the intervening period.

It is called a *balance sheet* because it is a measure of money flowing into and out of a 'closed system'. The money flowing into the system must equal the money possessed or flowing out. Or as we saw earlier, the total of debits must balance the total of credits.

Now let us look at a typical balance sheet. This first example is shown in the traditional style, with debits on one side and credits on the other. Most published accounts are now displayed in a vertical style which we will see later.

This example is the balance sheet of a fictional manufacturing company, Light Manufacturing Ltd. Note that the 'moment in time' — the date — is always given.

Example A

Balance sheet of Light Manufacturing Ltd
31st December 198X

		£'000			£'000
Share capital		200	*Fixed assets*		
			Land and buildings	75	
			Plant and machinery	85	
Reserves		50	Office equipment	20	
			Motor vehicles	30	
Long-term loans		160			210
			Current assets		
			Stocks	200	
Current liabilities			Debtors	120	
Creditors	120		Cash	5	
Bank overdraft	20				
		140			325
			Investments		15
		550			550

We can see from this balance sheet that, on the 31st December 198X, the assets of the company stood at £550,000, and included all the major categories — fixed assets, current assets and investments.

In the sources of finance, the left hand side, we see the share capital, loan capital and reserves as identified in the previous section. In addition, we can see that current liabilities are also shown as sources of finance — creditors and bank overdraft. Whilst strictly speaking they do represent short-term sources of finance, current liabilities are also part of the working finance of the company. The current liabilities are therefore often deducted from the current assets, and the balance sheet restated as follows.

Example B

Balance sheet of Light Manufacturing Ltd
31st December 198X

	£'000			£'000
Share capital	200	*Fixed assets*		
		Land and buildings	75	
		Plant and machinery	85	
Reserves	50	Office equipment	20	
		Motor vehicles	30	
Long-term loans	160			210
		Current assets		
		Stocks	200	
		Debtors	120	
		Cash	5	
			325	
		Less: Current liabilities		
		Creditors	(120)	
		Bank overdraft	(20)	
			(140)	
		Net current assets		185
		Investments		15
	410			410

6.2 The balance sheet — vertical style

The vertical-style balance sheet merely represents a change in presentation. The easiest way of explaining the presentation is through an exercise which involves completing a vertical balance sheet framework.

Exercise 4

In order to check your understanding of the balance sheet items, you will now use the information contained in the balance sheet above (Example B) to construct a vertical-style balance sheet. First of all enter the following items from the balance sheet above in the boxes:

continued

	£'000		£'000
Asset values		*Capital*	
Plant and machinery	[ ]	Reserves	[ ]
Stocks	[ ]	Long-term loan	[ ]
Liabilities:			
Creditors	[ ]		

Now complete the balance sheet format below:

Balance sheet of Light Manufacturing Ltd
31st December 198X

	£'000	£'000
Fixed assets		
Land and buildings	75	
Plant and machinery	[ ]	
Office equipment	20	
Motor vehicles	30	
		210
Long-term investments		15
Current assets		
Stocks	[ ]	
Debtors	120	
Cash	5	
	325	
Less: Current liabilities		
Creditors	[( )]	
Bank overdraft	(20)	
	(140)	
Net current assets		185
Total net assets employed:		410
		£'000
Financed by:		
Owners' equity		
Share capital	200	
Reserves	[ ]	
		250
Long-term loans		[ ]
		410

Now check your answer with that provided at the back of the book.

6.3 The annual report balance sheet statement

In an annual report, the current period balance sheet is always accompanied by the previous period's balance sheet. In this way a comparison between the two statements can be made, and the movements during the intervening period reviewed.

In order to demonstrate the full format we will once again use an exercise to both test your understanding of the balance sheet items, and show a full balance sheet statement as would appear in an annual report.

Exercise 5

A year has passed in the life of Light Manufacturing Ltd and we are now preparing the accounts as at 31st December 198Y.

You are requested:

(a) To calculate the new balance sheet totals, by taking the values at 31st December 198X and adjusting for the movement during the year. The first two items are completed to show how this is done.

(b) The new values are to be entered in the balance sheet format which follows.

(a) **Movements by balance sheet item during the year to 31/12/8Y**

Item	*Balance 31/12/8X £'000*	*Net Movement £'000*	*Balance 31/12/8Y £'000*
Fixed assets			
Land and buildings	75	nil	75
Plant and machinery	85	+ 20	105
Office equipment	20	nil	
Motor vehicles	30	+ 5	
Investments	15	nil	
Current assets and liabilities			
Stocks	200	– 20	
Debtors	120	+ 30	
Cash	5	nil	
Creditors	(120)	+(10)[more]	( )
Bank overdraft	(20)	–(15)[less]	( )
Share capital	200	nil	
Reserves (Movement in year's profit)	50	+ 40	
Long-term loan	160	nil	

continued

(b) Now using these new values complete the balance sheet format below.

Balance sheet of Light Manufacturing Ltd
as at 31st December 198Y

	198Y		*198X*	
	£'000	*£'000*	*£'000*	*£'000*
Fixed assets				
Land and buildings			75	
Plant and machinery			85	
Office equipment			20	
Motor vehicles			30	
				210
Long-term investments				15
Current assets				
Stocks			200	
Debtors			120	
Cash			5	
			325	
Less: Current liabilities				
Creditors	( )		(120)	
Bank overdraft	( )		(20)	
	( )		(140)	
Net current assets				185
Total net assets employed:				410
Financed by:				
Owners' equity				
Share capital			200	
Reserves			50	
				250
Long-term loan				160
				410

Once you are familiar with this, you will be able to understand most balance sheets. Each one is based on the format shown overleaf. They may be more complex in that they may have, for example, three types of share capital and several types of reserves, but the categories will be the same.

CHAPTER 7

The concept of value:

The need for depreciation, revaluation and provisions

This chapter introduces the concept of *value* and the factors which cause actual changes in asset values. It then goes on to explain the role of *depreciation* and *revaluation* in changing reported asset values.

7.1 The concept of value

So far, we have seen how a simple balance sheet is created on the basis of money supplied and money spent. The problem which then occurs is that, once purchased, our fixed assets will change in value.

Consider these examples:

- The *land* owned by a company may well increase in value, unless we are in the mining or quarrying business, in which case the property may become exhausted and of zero value
- The company's *buildings* may increase in value in the short term, but will eventually deteriorate and require replacement or modernization
- *Plant and machinery* may wear out, become obsolete, or just too expensive to maintain (i.e. be uneconomic). In time, they only have value as scrap
- As well as losing value as soon as they are purchased, *vehicles* become uneconomic to run after a time.

But it is not only fixed assets that change in value. *Stocks* of raw materials, components or finished goods may be similarly affected. Most of us are familiar with the following occurrences.

- Materials or parts purchased in quantities far in excess of foreseeable usage.
- Stocks held of components that have been superceded (replaced by others that are better or cheaper)
- Stocks held for a product no longer manufactured, or stocks of a product no longer sold
- Stocks which have deteriorated over time and are now not fit for use.

In each of these occurrences, the value of the stock will diminish. Of course, the opposite may also happen. Each time the price of a product goes up, stocks of finished goods become more valuable. A prime example of this is provided by petrol filling stations, whose stock of petrol can rise in value overnight on the announcement of a price increase.

Finally, even the debtors value shown on the balance sheet will not necessarily be an accurate reflection of the money that can be collected over time. Some of our customers will go bankrupt, and some dispute the quantity or quality of goods supplied. Because of this, it will normally be impossible to collect 100 per cent of the goods invoiced as cash.

These changes in value have to be recognized in financial accounts so that the *actual* wealth of the company can be reported. The changes have to be handled in different ways according to the *type* of asset. We will now review how these changes are made for each asset type.

7.2 Fixed assets — the need for depreciation

In most cases, fixed assets reduce in value over time as they gradually wear out. Therefore, unless we make an adjustment to lower the original cost figure shown in the accounts, we will be overstating the value of the asset. Furthermore, if the value of assets *is* overstated, the balancing value of the shareholders' investment will be overstated by the same amount.

This is illustrated in the following simplified example in which we see how the accounts of a taxi driver setting out in business would reflect changes in the value of a major asset over time.

The business starts with £5,000 share capital provided by the owner. This capital is used to purchase a taxi. The opening balance sheet year in year 1 would be:

Opening balance sheet

Share capital	£5,000	*Motor vehicle*	£5,000

During the following three years, he operates on a cash basis — he has neither debtors nor creditors. In addition, after paying his salary and all his expenses, he generates a cash surplus of £1,500 each year. What would his balance sheet look like at the end of the three years?

Balance sheet at the end of year 3

	£		£
Share capital	5,000	*Motor vehicle*	5,000
Reserves (3×£1,500)	4,500	*Bank balace*	4,500
	9,500		9,500

It appears that the taxi driver's shareholding is now worth £9,500, as represented by the assets. However, the taxi shown as the fixed asset is now worth say, only £2,500. In reality therefore the assets are worth only:

Motor vehicle	£2,500	
Bank balance	£4,500	
		£7,000

If the asset value is reduced, a corresponding reduction in profit has to be made to complete the double entry. The adjusted balance sheet appears as follows:

Balance sheet at the end of year 3

	£		£
Share capital	5,000	*Motor vehicle*	2,500
Reserves	2,000	*Bank balance*	4,500
	7,000		7,000

This means that the asset value has been adjusted to reflect the changing value of the asset, and the shareholders funds reduced to give a more accurate reflection of the company's worth.

7.3 The calculation of depreciation

The way in which this reduction in fixed asset value is reflected in accounts is called *depreciation*.

In order to establish a standard method of calculating depreciation, we have to redefine our view of the capital expenditure made in purchasing an asset as follows:

The capital payment for an asset is a payment in advance for the use of the asset over its useful lifetime.

Therefore, a proportion of the capital outlay is charged as an expense against the profits earned by the asset over its lifetime.

In other words, a depreciation charge is made each year which, over the life of the asset, is equal to the capital outlay. Again, let us use an example to illustrate how depreciation operates.

Our company purchases a packaging machine for £9,000. We are advised that the machine will be used in packaging a product that will be withdrawn in four years' time. The machine will not be suitable for the replacement product, but it will be worth £1,000 as scrap at that time. How do we calculate the depreciation charge? How is the charge shown in the accounts?

Our first step is to calculate the *depreciable amount* (the amount of value lost during the useful life) which is equal to:

Original cost — Residual value

Which, in our example, is:

£9,000 – £1,000 = £8,000

Original cost – *Residual value (Scrap value)* = *Depreciable amount*

Step two is to spread the depreciable amount over the useful life of the asset. This is done by dividing the *depreciable amount* by the *estimated life* to give the *annual depreciation charge*:

Annual depreciation charge or provision

$$= \frac{\text{Depreciable amount}}{\text{Useful life}} \text{ or } \frac{£8{,}000}{4 \text{ years}}$$

$$= £2{,}000 \text{ per annum}$$

In summary, if we charge £2,000 per annum for four years against profit, we can reduce the value of the machine from £9,000 (its original purchase price) to £1,000, its estimated scrap value at that time.

In practice, companies often have a preset depreciation life for similar types of assets. For example, all computers may be given an estimated life of four years because they become obsolete quickly. Heavy structural plant items, on the other hand, may be depreciated over 20 years.

Assets are usually depreciated in one of two ways: the *straight-line* basis, which was shown above, or the *reducing balance* basis. The reducing balance method involves depreciating an asset by a fixed percentage on the balance outstanding at the start of the period. The value of annual depreciation reduces each year under this second method which is often a better reflection of what happens to values in real life.

A comparison of the two methods is shown below. The straight-line calculation is based on the example given above. The reducing-balance calculation is based on the purchase value of £9,000 and is at a rate that will give a residual value of about £1,000 after four years.

	Straight-line basis			*Reducing-balance basis*		
Rate:	25% of depreciable amount			40% of starting value		
Year	*Start value*	*Depreciation amount*	*End value*	*Start value*	*Depreciation amount*	*End value*
	£	£	£	£	£	£
1	9,000	2,000	7,000	9,000	3,600	5,400
2	7,000	2,000	5,000	5,400	2,160	3,240
3	5,000	2,000	3,000	3,240	1,296	1,944
4	3,000	2,000	1,000	1,944	778	1,166

As you can see, the second method generates a higher depreciation in the early years.

7.4 Depreciation in the accounts

The way that depreciation is reflected in the accounts is not affected by the calculation method, it is just the amount that will vary. The depreciation charge for our packaging machine is reflected in the accounts as follows (using the straight-line amounts). (N.B. For simplicity we assume that it is the only asset.):

Balance sheet before the depreciation charge

Share capital	£9,000	*Fixed asset*	£9,000
Reserves	£3,000	*Cash*	£3,000
	£12,000		£12,000

If we make a depreciation charge of £2,000 for the year the balance sheet becomes:

Revised balance sheet after depreciation charge

Share capital	£9,000	*Fixed asset*	£9,000	
		Less: Depreciation	£2,000	
				£7,000
Reserves	£1,000	*Cash*		£3,000
	£10,000			£10,000

Note that the reserves have also reduced by £2,000, because of the charge made against profit. This charge completes the double-entry in the books and reduces the profit retained and transferred to reserves. The reduced value of the asset is known as the *written-down value* or *net book value*.

In each of the four years, the depreciation charge against the asset value will be increased by £2,000. The total amount is known as *accumulated depreciation*.

At the same time, if the company makes £3,000 per year *before* charging depreciation, the year 4 balance sheet will appear as follows:

Balance sheet at the end of year 4

Share capital	$9,000	*Fixed asset*	$9,000	
		Less: Depreciation	$8,000	
				$1,000
Reserves (4×$1,000)	$4,000	*Cash* (4×$3,000)		$12,000
	$13,000			$13,000

So, at the end of year 4, the net book value of the machine is recorded as $1,000, which, if our estimates were correct, can now be realized by selling the machine for scrap.

Before leaving this example, it is worth looking at how the balance sheet would appear if no depreciation had been charged:

Balance sheet at the end of year 4 (without depreciation)

Share capital	$9,000	*Fixed asset*	$9,000
Reserves (4×$3,000)	$12,000	*Cash* (4×$3,000)	$12,000
	$21,000		$21,000

Thus, the balance sheet shows an asset value of $9,000 and a — company worth $21,000, both of which are overstated by $8,000 — the accumulated depreciation.

The other problem with this approach is that it would probably lead to more profit being distributed as dividend, instead of being transferred to reserves. As this would also lead to a reduction in the cash balance, it would affect the company's ability to purchase new equipment.

7.5 Revaluation of assets

We have seen how fixed assets that *reduce* in value are dealt with. Traditionally, all assets, with the exception of land, are depreciated, with land being held in the books at cost. This practice has led, in some circumstances, to an *understatement* of asset values, and, in particular, the values of land and buildings.

In the 1960s and 1970s, for example, the sharp rises in land and property prices led to many companies having undervalued land and property assets on their books. This, of course, also meant that share prices tended to be undervalued. As a consequence, many companies were taken over by firms specializing in 'asset stripping'. Asset stripping meant closing or transferring

operations being carried out in the undervalued property assets, and then selling the property assets for a quick profit.

It is now usual to revalue property assets on a more regular basis, using professional valuers. The values in the accounts are then adjusted to realistic current levels, and a balancing entry made to reserves using a specific revaluation reserve. To demonstrate how this works in practice we will take the example of a company with a sole asset — freehold land — bought originally for £20,000, but now valued at £30,000. The balance sheet at the end of 198X was as follows:

Share capital	£10,000	*Fixed asset*	£20,000
Reserves	£10,000		
	£20,000		£20,000

The revised balance sheet incorporating the revaluation is:

Share capital		£10,000	*Fixed asset*	£30,000
Reserves				
P&L	£10,000			
Revaluation	£10,000			
		£20,000		
		£30,000		£30,000

Exercise 6

To return to Light Manufacturing Ltd, the original fixed asset values shown at 31st December 198X were:

	£'000
Land and buildings	75
Plant and machinery	85
Office equipment	20
Motor vehicles	30
	210

continued

These figures actually represented written-down values, the full entries being:

Fixed asset category	*Cost*	*Accumulated depreciation*	*Net book value*
	£'000	*£'000*	*£'000*
Land and buildings	75	nil	75
Plant and machinery	200	115	85
Office equipment	40	20	20
Motor vehicles	65	35	30
	380	170	210

In this case, it has been assumed that land and buildings are not depreciated.

During 198Y Light Manufacturing made the following capital expenditure purchases (no sales were made):

- A new production line was completed at the following cost during the year:

	£
Drills and presses	£25,000
Conveyors	£7,000
Finishing machines	£10,000
Total	£42,000

- New office equipment cost £4,000
- Three new delivery vans costing £5,000 each were purchased together with an extra car for a new salesman at £4,000.

(a) Calculate the new *cost* totals as at 31st December 198Y using the following table:

Fixed asset category	*Cost 31/12/8X*	*Additions during 198Y*	*Cost 31/12/8Y*
	£'000	*£'000*	*£'000*
Land and buildings	75	nil	75
Plant and machinery	200		
Office equipment	40		
Motor vehicles	65		
	380		

We have also been informed that the depreciation charge for the year was £40,000; split £22,000 plant and machinery, £4,000 office equipment, and £14,000 on motor vehicles.

(b) Complete the depreciation table below.

Fixed asset category	*Accumulated depreciation 31/12/8X £'000*	*Depreciation charged during 198Y £'000*	*Accumulated depreciation 31/12/8Y £'000*
Land and buildings	nil	nil	nil
Plant and machinery	115		
Office equipment	20		
Motor vehicles	35		
	170	40	210

(c) Finally, you are now in a position to calculate the full fixed assets schedule for the 198Y balance sheet.

Fixed asset category	*Cost at 31/12/8Y £'000*	*Accumulated depreciation 31/12/8Y £'000*	*Net book value 31/12/8Y £'000*
Land and buildings			
Plant and machinery			
Office equipment			
Motor vehicles			

7.6 Stock and work in progress values

Some people reading this book will be familiar with physical stocktakes. At stocktake times, the stock quantities and values shown in the accounts and in stock records are checked by physically counting the actual quantities and establishing their real worth.

As mentioned earlier, it is important to identify excess, obsolete or valueless stocks in the course of stocktaking so that we do not continue to hold them in the accounts as assets of value.

Specifically identified items of stock that are of zero value are *written off* as a charge to the profit and loss account. This allows the stock total to be reduced by the same amount. In cases where a tight stock control system is not in place, it is normal to reduce the value of stocks held by creating a general *stock provision* of, say, 5 per cent of the total value of stocks. In this way, a provision is made for valueless stock not so far specifically identified.

7.7 Debtor values

The value of debtors (or *receivables*) has to be periodically verified in a similar way to stock. In this way we can check that the amounts shown as owing to us are still collectable — that the customer is both willing and able to pay. Specific bad debts have to be written off when it is clear that the customer will never pay — for example, if he is declared bankrupt.

It is usual to create a general provision to cover the small proportion of the remaining debt that we assume will also never be paid. This provision is based on judgement, taking into account previous experience and the amount of long outstanding and disputed debt.

7.8 Measurement of value

So far in this chapter, we have been reviewing the standard ways in which accountants cope with the changing values of assets. But the obvious question still remains, why follow this standard procedure? Why don't we simply value each asset prior to completion of the balance sheet?

The principal answer to this is that value varies according to the *perception of the valuer.* We can illustrate this by taking an example of a commonly owned asset and seeing how different individuals might value it. The example we will use is a company car which cost £7,500 three years ago, and is being used by a salesman. The valuations are as follows:

- *The sales manager's view*

The sales manager will be chiefly concerned with *deprival value* — for example, if the car is taken away the salesman may lose sales worth, say,

£20,000 a month

In a similar way, a cost accountant or cost engineer may consider the *economic value* of an asset — the value which the company earns from the use of an asset.

- *The treasury accountant*

The treasury accountant is concerned with the cash requirements of the company, so he may well be concerned with financing a *replacement* car. He will calculate the *replacement value* and the *expected sale price* in order to calculate a funding figure.

Replacement value — £9,000
Sale value — £1,500
Net funding needed — £7,500

- *The financial accountant*

The financial accountant may use the depreciation method discussed earlier, and will depreciate the car to zero value over, say, five years. At the end of three years, the car will have a net book value of:

£7,500 – £7,500 × 3/5
£3,500

- *The finance company*

If, instead of purchasing the vehicle outright, we had purchased the car on a three-year lease, we would just have paid the final installment on the car, and the value to the finance company would be:

Zero

- *Finally, the car dealer*

The car dealer will normally have at least two values in mind — a purchase price and a selling price. These could be as follows:

Purchase price — £1,500
Sales price — £3,000

What is the real value?

- Exceptional for its year
- Only one owner
- Not a scratch!
- Average mileage

£3,000

- Not much demand for these
- A company car!
- Not A1 condition
- Mileage!

£1,500

As we have seen, the value of an asset can be determined in many different ways, with various people giving widely differing views! If valuation became the major method of fixing the price of assets in accounts, comparison of the accounts of different companies would become almost impossible. The cost-less-depreciation method may be cumbersome, but at least it is consistent.

Other methods have been, and are still being, considered by the accounting authorities. Some companies want to include the value of their product brands as assets. The problem is that a level of consistency is required in valuation techniques so that all company accounts are prepared in the same way. Any change in accounting methods has to be applicable to *all* businesses.

In this chapter, we have investigated the ways in which financial accounts reflect changing asset values. The assets of a company represent a prime source of wealth, both in their intrinsic values and in their capacity to earn profits. Proper maintenance and good management of assets are the hallmarks of all successful companies. We will return to the importance of asset management later in the book, as it is one of the key factors in modern company management.

CHAPTER 8

The financial reports Part 2

This chapter deals with the remaining statements that form a key part of company accounts; the *profit and loss account*, the *source and application of funds statement*, and the *statement of added value*.

Earlier in the book, we examined the balance sheet as one of the major accounts statements. We now turn to another of these statements — the profit and loss account.

8.1 The profit and loss account

Whereas the balance sheet measures a company's wealth at a moment in time, the profit and loss or P&L account measures the activity occurring over a period of time. Obviously, the P&L account normally covers the annual period between successive balance sheet dates, and provides information on the major revenue (sales) and cost movements occurring which result in the retained earnings figure.

In order to demonstrate this more clearly we will examine Light Manufacturing Ltd's profit and loss transactions occurring in the year ending 31st December 198Y — between the two balance sheet dates. We already know from a previous exercise (see p. 38) that the transfer to reserves (retained earnings) was £40,000. We shall now see how this profit figure was produced.

For the sake of clarity, the profit and loss account will be shown first as it is assembled, then as it usually appears in company annual reports, the latter being an abbreviated version of the full account.

Light Manufacturing Ltd:
Profit and loss account for the year ended 31st December 198Y (In full)

	£'000	*£'000*
Sales turnover		600
Less: *Cost of sales*:		
Opening stocks	200	
Manufacturing costs	*Add*:	
Materials purchased	100	
Production labour	130	
Manufacturing expenses	50	
	480	
Less: *Closing stocks*	180	
		(300)
Gross profit		300
Less: *Other costs*		
Selling and distribution	90	
Administration	50	
Depreciation	40	

	£'000	£'000
		180
* *Trading profit*		120
Add: Income from investments		2
Less: Interest on long term loan		20
* *Profit before tax*		102
Less: Taxation		40
* *Profit after tax*		62
Less: Dividends		22
* Retained profit (Transferred to reserves)		40

Note
The asterisk (*) indicates five profit definitions, each different. You should always check what is meant when 'profit' is referred to. Also note that costs charged in the year are those matching sales, the costs incurred in making closing stocks are held over until the products are sold.

Light Manufacturing Ltd:
Profit and loss account for the year ended
31st December 198Y (As published)

	£'000
Sales turnover	600
Trading profit	120
Income from investments	2
	122
Interest charges	20
Profit before taxation	102
Taxation	40
Profit after taxation	62
Appropriation: Dividends paid	22
Retained profit	40

As you can see, the published accounts, although derived from the operating expenses, show little detail.

Exercise 7

You are required to construct a P&L statement for Light Manufacturing Ltd, relating to the year ended 31st December 198X. The format to be used is the published basis. However, there is an initial working format to be completed to calculate the trading profit. The following data is relevant.

	£'000
Cost of sales (after stock adjustment)	250
Taxation	35
Dividends paid	15
Sales turnover	500
Other costs (selling, admin. etc.)	160
Income from investments	2
Interest charges	17

Working format:		*£'000*
Sales turnover		
Less: Cost of sales		
other costs		
Trading profit		

Light Manufacturing Ltd:
Profit and loss account for the year ended
31st December 198X (Published account format)

	£'000
Sales turnover	
Trading profit	
Income from investments	
Interest charges	
Profit before taxation	
Less: Taxation	
Profit after taxation	
Appropriation: Dividends paid	
Retained profit	

8.2 The source and application of funds statement

We have seen how the balance sheet records wealth at a moment in time and how the profit and loss account provides detail of the movement of that wealth between balance sheet dates. This information is supplemented in the annual accounts by the *source and application of funds* or *funds flow statement*. The role of this statement is to track the sources and uses of funds in the period under review.

It is a crucial document because the cash position of a company is of fundamental importance to its continuing existence. Companies go out of business if they run out of cash, and cannot pay their bills. This does not happen when a company fails to make a profit, although, of course, the two are connected and operation at a loss may well lead to a cash crisis. Funds flow statements are also very important in planning for the future. The same format can be used for either past or future figures. Funds flow statements are prepared as follows:

Funds inflows
The first step is to identify *all* the sources of income, in other words, all the money flowing into the company. In a mature company, the principal source of money is from retained earnings, i.e., revenue earned less costs incurred. We start the funds flow statement therefore with the profit before tax figure. Next, we must adjust this figure to take account of all the charges made in the profit and loss account which do not involve cash movements. The main examples of this are depreciation and provisions. Then we add the money received from other sources such as:

- from further share issues
- from bank loans or other borrowings
- from the sale of fixed assets

which gives us *total funds generated*.

Use of funds
We now need to list the usage of funds by type of expenditure. The following are typical of expenditure usually shown:

- Capital expenditure — fixed assets purchased.
- Investments made.
- Payments to the Inland Revenue (the taxman), and shareholders. These payments are not necessarily the amounts shown in the P&L account, as both dividends and taxation may be partially or wholly paid at a later date. The amounts outstanding as liabilities at the end of the year will be shown on the balance sheet as creditors. The figures paid out in the current year may well therefore relate to the previous year's P&L figures.

Finally, we show the movements of funds used in working capital. Increases in working assets or decreases in liabilities involve the use of extra funds, whilst decreases in assets and increases in liabilities represent the release of funds. The movements in working capital funds are measured by calculating the changes in asset and liability totals between successive balance sheets.

For example, in the balance sheet produced in Exercise 5 (p. 39), the stock value for 198Y is £180,000 compared with £200,000 in 198X. This represents a reduction in the funds required to finance stock of £20,000, or a release of funds to this value.

We should now be in the situation that the total funds generated equal the funds used and we have completed the statement. We will now view the full statement as prepared for Light Manufacturing Ltd.

Note
In some cases, a different order of presentation is used in which the final line represents the increase or reduction in borrowings.

Light Manufacturing Ltd
Funds flow statement for the year ended 31st December 198Y

		£'000
Sources of funds		
Profit before taxation		102
Add: Non-cash item depreciation		40
Funds from other sources		nil
Total funds generated		142
Uses of funds (applications)		
Capital expenditure		65
Dividends paid		15
Taxation paid		35
Working capital movements:		
Increase(decrease) in funds used		
Reduction in stocks	(20)	
Increase in debtors	30	
Decrease in trade creditors	2	
Reduced bank overdraft	15	
		27
		142

Note
The dividend and taxation payments used are those for the year ended December 198X. The creditor movement shown has therefore been restricted to trade creditors only, the taxation and dividend creditors can be ignored.

From this schedule we can see that the company was able to reduce the bank overdraft by £15,000 in the year.

Exercise 8

Given the following information relating to Light Manufacturing for the year to 31st December 198X, complete the funds flow statement shown below.

Information for the year	*£'000*
Stock values increased by	20
Capital expenditure totalled	55
Assets sold realized	10
Dividends paid	15
Taxation paid	30
Profit before tax	75
Depreciation charged	35
Debtors increased by	10
Trade creditors increased by	5
The bank overdraft rose by	5

Light Manufacturing Ltd
Funds flow statement for the year ended
31st December 198X

		£'000
Sources of funds		
Profit before taxation		
Add: Non-cash item depreciation		
Funds from other sources: Sales of assets		
Total funds generated		
Uses of funds (applications)		
Capital expenditure		
Dividends paid		
Taxation paid		
Working capital movements:		
(Increase/(decrease) in funds used)		
Increase in stocks		
Increase in debtors		
Increase in trade creditors	( )	
Increased bank overdraft	( )	
Total funds used		

8.3 The statement of value added

The statement of value added is not published in all company accounts. What it represents is an alternative way of showing wealth created by a company during a financial period. In addition, it shows the way in which the wealth is distributed. It is valuable in explaining to employees and shareholders how the wealth, which they have helped create, is shared out.

The wealth created or *value added* is the difference between the sales achieved and the cost of goods and services purchased. In other words, it is the value added through the efforts of the employees using the capital and facilities of the business.

The basic figures are produced by a reworking of the figures used in the profit and loss account. The first step is to identify the inputs to the company — the goods and services purchased.

For Light Manufacturing Ltd, this is calculated as follows:

		Cost allocation	
Category	*Value*	*Bought*	*Added*
	£'000	*£'000*	*£'000*
Cost of sales	300	160	140
Selling and distribution	90	30	60
Administration	50	20	30
Depreciation	40	nil	40
	480	210	270

So, what we have done is to include all the purchased materials (raw materials, components, packaging, etc.) together with services purchased (rents, heat, light, advertising etc.) in the purchased column.

In the added value column, we are left with the labour costs, and costs associated with capital such as depreciation.

Our value added can then be calculated as follows:

	£'000
Total value of goods produced: (Sales turnover)	600
Less: Materials and services supplied by others	210
Value added	390

The full value added statement can now be completed by demonstrating how this value added has been distributed to the various contributors to wealth creation.

Light Manufacturing Ltd
Statement of value added for the year ended
31st December 198Y

	£'000	%
Sales turnover	600	
Less: Goods and services supplied by others	210	
Value added by trading operations	390	
Add: Investment income received	2	
Total wealth created	392	100
Used as follows:		
To employees: salaries, wages, pensions, etc.	230	59
To government: taxation	40	10
To lenders (banks etc.): interest	20	5
To shareholders: dividends	22	8
Retained for growth and investment	80	18
	392	100

Note
The amount retained for future growth is made up of depreciation and retained earnings.

8.4 Summary of the annual accounts schedules

You should now be familiar with the structure and content of the major financial reporting schedules as produced periodically by each trading company. These are:

- the balance sheet
- the profit and loss account
- the source and applications of funds statement
- the statement of value added.

The annual accounts of each limited company in the UK must, by law, contain at least the first two schedules, those of larger companies usually contain all of them.

Although we have tried to keep the examples simple, you will find that all company accounts broadly follow the formats we have described. So, whether you review international group accounts containing the combined results of worldwide operations or the accounts of a small two-man jobbing engineering company, the presentation will be similar.

We will review the presentation and content of the company annual reports and accounts later, but you may find it useful to compare the accounting schedules of any company reports available with our examples.

You may have observed that these annual accounts schedules are designed to satisfy the information needs of a number of different groups, most of which are external to the company — shareholders, lenders, analysts etc. Consequently, they do not contain the kind of timely detailed information required by internal management.

In addition, it is important to remember that the annual accounts are a record of *past* events. In order to run a business successfully, however, we need to make decisions concerned with the future.

We will now examine the detailed accounts required by management involved in the day-to-day running of the business.

PART 2

Part 2 Cost accounting

CHAPTER 9

The role of cost accounting

This chapter explains what cost and management accounts are and what they do. It also describes an approach to implementing a cost accounting system.

9.1 What are cost and management accounting?

Cost accounting is the means by which a company produces the day-to-day financial information needed by managers to run the business. You might ask why cost accounts are necessary when a company already keeps financial accounts. The reason is that the prime purpose of the financial accounts, as we have seen in earlier chapters, is to keep records and provide reports that satisfy the legal requirements imposed on the company and present essentially historic information. The internal requirements of a company for financial information mean that a separate system is required. This does not necessarily mean that an entirely independent system is required — the same basic financial information may still be used. Where it should differ is in its *relevance* to key activities and its timeliness, availability and style of presentation.

Cost accounting is likely to be the area of accounting with which you are most familiar. Aspects of cost accounting affect all management roles, irrespective of the department concerned. You may have been involved, for example, in setting cost standards, costing out products or processes, or keeping performance records. You may have dealt with measures and yardsticks used in cost accounting without ever having considered them as 'financial' measures.

It is difficult to describe where cost accounting ends and *management accounting* begins. *Management accounts* is the term used to describe the periodic reports prepared for management which are based on the cost accounts. In general, management accounts are a summarized form of the cost accounts which have been subjected to further analysis in order to emphasize any issues or concerns and explain unexpected trends.

9.2 What is the role of cost accounting?

The role of cost accounting is to identify the basic control factors used on a day-by-day basis in managing a business and to report on them as and when required. The basic control factors most frequently reported are:

- The revenue and costs associated with individual managers in the business, i.e. the sales and costs for which they are responsible, whether they be manager of:
  - ★ the company — responsible for total profit
  - ★ a factory — responsible for cost-effective production
  - ★ a department, a process or, an activity — responsible for efficient performance

  For example, a sales manager will be responsible for meeting both sales and cost targets, whereas a transport manager will be responsible for meeting delivery targets at an economic cost

- The efficiency, productivity and effectiveness of processes and services.

- The utilization of resources — manpower, plant and machinery, vehicles, buildings, cash, etc.

The need for cost accounting becomes greater as the size of a company increases. Obviously, the owner or manager of a small business can usually judge, using common sense or intuition, the state of the business. As a business grows, and top management become remote from the factory floor and authority is delegated, a control and reporting system becomes necessary to enable the managers to measure performance.

In the next few chapters, therefore, we will review the structure, form and use of cost accounts in providing such a control system.

9.3 The basics of cost accounting

Cost accounts, or the elements of cost accounts — standard costs, cost centres etc. — are the facets of accounting with which non-financial managers most commonly come into contact. This is because, in a well-run company, the cost accounting structure permeates the whole business, thus allowing management to keep track of day-to-day activities.

Because cost accounts have to be matched to an individual business, the structure of this function varies considerably from company to company. In addition, unlike financial accounts, there is no legal requirement to produce cost accounts in any particular form, or indeed at all (except, of course, the general need to demonstrate proper internal controls).

Cost accounts also differ from financial accounts in that, if they are to fulfil their role in everyday management, they must be *timely*. In some cases, the accuracy of the figures suffers because of the need to provide figures promptly. In other words, it is often better for management to receive 90 per cent accurate figures, five days after the end of a month, than 100 per cent accurate figures after three months.

Over the years, however, some methods have been developed for cost accounting which are commonly used in most industries. We will be investigating the most frequently occurring types. There is no formal requirement for cost accounts to be audited. However, the need for management to demonstrate that adequate internal controls exist means that the auditors may well wish to check that systems are in place and do produce reasonably accurate information.

9.4 Implementing cost accounts

In setting up a cost accounting system, the factors that most affect the approach taken are:

- the information required by management (by product, process etc.)

- the manner in which responsibility is delegated (by department, location, group or individual)
- the type of industry or business in which the company operates
- the types of costs that are incurred.

Thus, in planning a company costing system, the approach has to be from the two ends of the business simultaneously. That is, from the top downwards, in terms of information required, and from the bottom up, in terms of information available.

The following diagram illustrates this:

Figure 2: The costing system

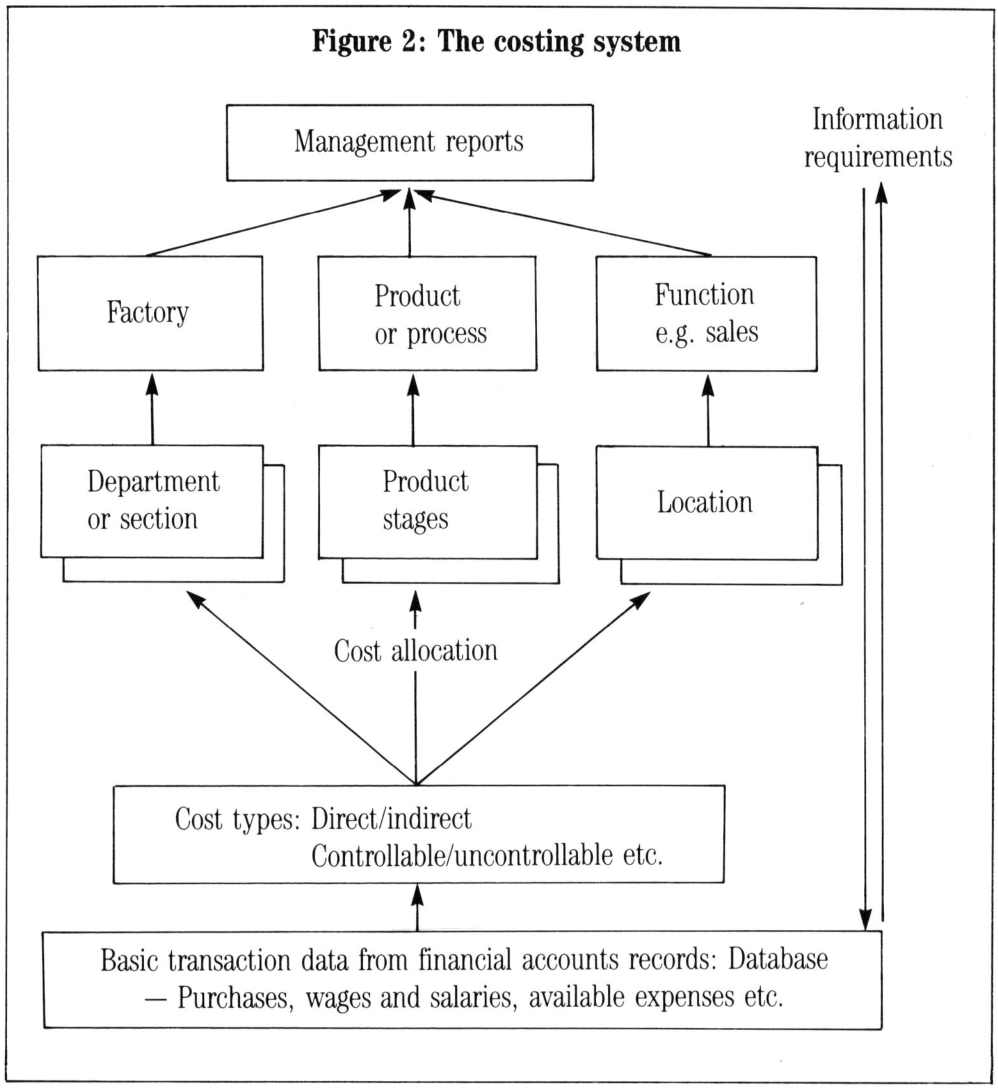

Cost accounting systems normally rely on the basic financial accounting records as the source of cost information. Such systems are known as *integrated accounting systems*.

The way that the twin systems of cost accounts (including budgeting) and financial accounts can permeate a company are shown in the diagram on the next page.

Figure 3: The hierarchy of accounts

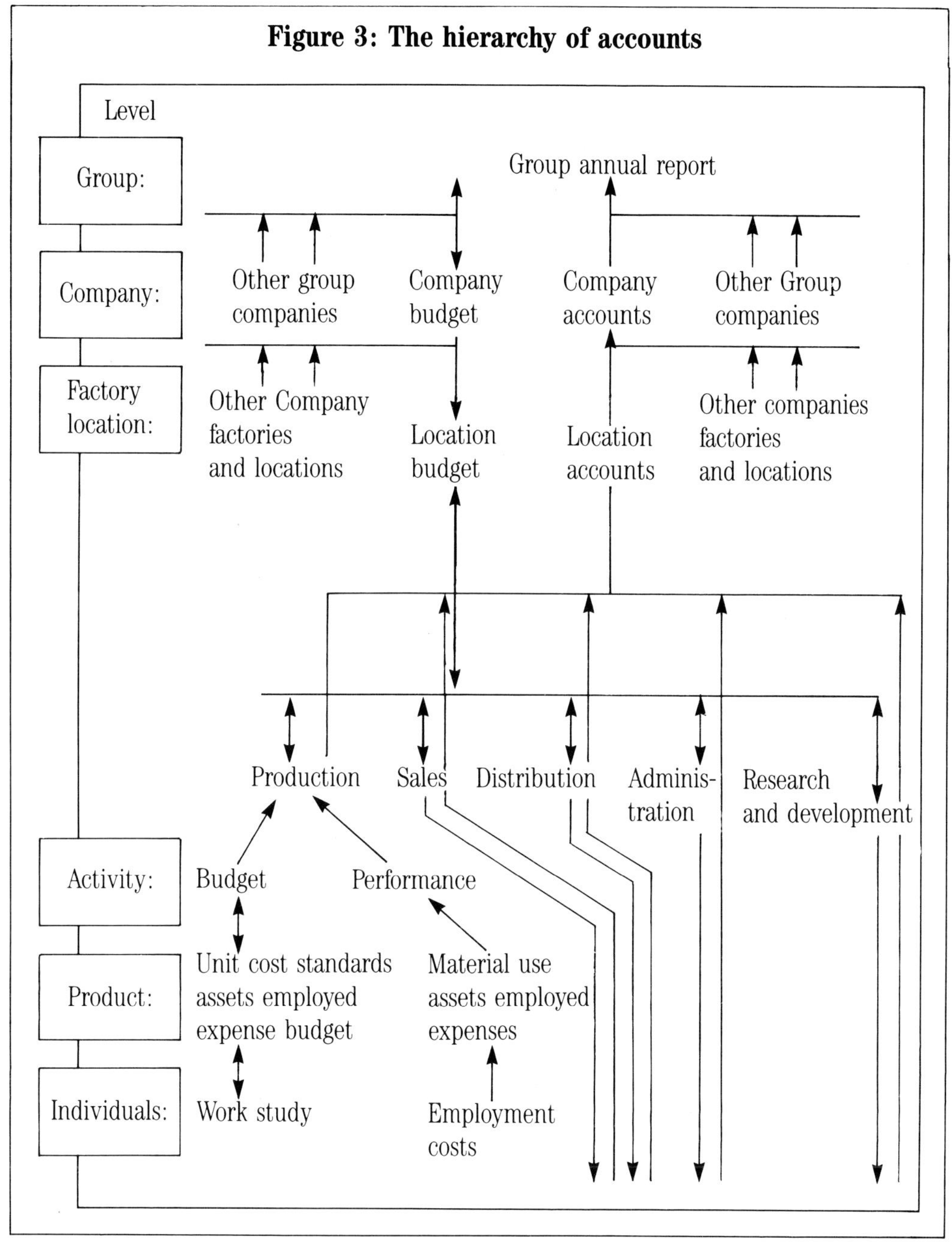

Note that, for the sake of clarity, only production department activity is indicated. Other departments, such as distribution and sales, have their own specific measures. In addition to the formal management reporting requirements, the cost accounts form the source of information for *ad hoc* requirements such as product pricing, machine replacement, manpower deployment and so on. Costing system design must also recognize these uses.

Exercise 9

Answer the following statements by stating whether they are true or false (write *T* or *F*).

(a) Cost accounts, like annual financial report statements, have to be produced in a standard format.

____

(b) Cost accounts unlike financial accounts use non-financial factors such as measurement of manpower hours.

____

(c) Sometimes it is better to sacrifice 100% accuracy with cost accounts in order to produce timely reports.

____

(d) Cost accounts are much more concerned with external reporting.

____

(e) The presentation of financial accounts is largely determined by internal management needs.

____

(f) When the financial and cost accounts derive from a common information base the system is known as an integrated system.

____

(g) The role of cost accounts is to reflect the basic control factors in a business.

____

(h) Auditors must validate the cost accounts system.

____

CHAPTER 10

Management information requirements

This chapter demonstrates how cost accounting systems are structured in a way that suits the management information requirements of the organization.

10.1 Responsibilities

A key factor in running a business is the delegation of responsibility. For such delegation to work well, there should be a control system for checking performance which can be provided by a cost accounts facility.

The first step in setting up any costing system is to research and define what the managers need to know in order to control the business. These information needs are likely to fall into two major categories:

- **Personal** — connected with the performance of individuals.
- **Impersonal** — associated with the measurement of products, locations or processes.

To take the former category, each manager in the organization should have responsibility for the expenditure and/or income in the area under his or her command. These financial responsibilities may be defined as any (or all) of the following:

- Revenue
- Costs
- Profit
- Investment.

10.2 Personal cost centres

Performance against these responsibilities is measured in practice by allocating a *personal cost centre* to the manager concerned. In this way, all income produced and expenditure incurred can be attributed directly to the department or area under his or her responsibility. (*Note* — Cost centre structure is also dealt with later in this chapter.)

A cost centre is created by giving a unique number to the person's department or area and then allocating all relevant income or expenditure to that person's number.

Consider some examples:

- A managing director is responsible for a profit and investment centre. In other words, he is accountable for *sales income less costs* which, of course, is profit, and the use of capital provided to the company. He will normally delegate his authority to reporting directors, their managers and so on down through the organization. Nevertheless, he will retain ultimate responsibility for the performance of the company.
- A sales manager is responsible for the achievement of sales revenue — a 'revenue' cost centre. In addition, he must manage the departmental costs, so the sales manager is also responsible for a 'cost' cost centre. In some companies, the sales manager will be 'charged' by the production manager or factory for the cost of products sold. The sales department then becomes a profit centre.

- A factory or production line manager controls a profit centre in which 'sales income' is the transfer price of goods to the sales department. Production costs can then be reviewed against this 'income'.

The extension of *cost* centres into *profit* centres is used to give a sharper commercial perspective to the relevant managers. This practice is also quite common with service departments such as, for example, a computer department. If the computer department is allowed to charge users at commercial rates, the departmental manager can then be held responsible for holding computer costs to a level at which the department makes a profit.

10.3 Investment centres

An *investment* centre is one where, in addition to normal cost responsibilities, the manager has authority over the investment in, and use of, assets. A transport manager, for example, might have authority for the purchase of vehicles, and the production manager for new machinery and equipment.

The responsibility for investment can be delegated in a similar way to the revenue and expenditure costs. As investment decisions often involve large sums of money, and the implications of these decisions usually last for many years, *capital expenditure approval* should be rigidly controlled. The control and evaluation of investment is dealt with in greater detail later.

10.4 Impersonal cost centres

In addition to the requirement for information by personal responsibility, managers often require information to be allocated to *impersonal cost centres* — an area or item that represents no one individual's responsibility, for example these could be:

- a location
- a process or operation
- a product.

These cost centres may replace the personal cost centres or, more likely, be additional to them.

If we take the example of a manufacturing company with a production line capable of producing three different products, it is likely that management will be interested in profitability by product as well as by the total production cost. The figures in the table below show how we can measure the overall performance of the production line (hence the production manager) and demonstrate the performance of the department by product.

Month 3 manufacturing results for XYZ

Item	*Production line total £'000*	*Product 1 £'000*	*Product 2 £'000*	*Product 3 £'000*
Value of output (at transfer prices)	180	100	50	30
Costs				
Labour	85	50	20	15
Materials	45	30	10	5
Expenses	15	5	5	5
Overheads	18	10	5	3
Profit	17	5	10	2
	Production manager's cost centre	Product cost centres		

The creation of cost centres must reflect the requirements of management in managing both people and products or processes. Each business will need to identify its own particular needs. A car manufacturer, for instance, would primarily be interested in cost and profit per car produced. On the other hand, in an engineering business, cost per contract could be the main management yardstick.

10.5 Selection of the costing method

The selection of impersonal cost centres has a major bearing on the way the cost accounting process is carried out. The key to this process is the *cost unit* which management identifies as its key control measure.

If the chosen unit is the cost of an individual product or service as it is with most companies producing and selling large quantities of identical or homogeneous products or services, *operations*, *unit* or *process costings* are used. These methods, which are basically similar, involve finding out the total costs incurred in manufacturing a particular product or operating a service and then averaging the costs over the units of output to give a unit cost.

This method is suitable for discrete products such as headlamps, bricks, bread, and even oil (cost per barrel being the unit). It also applies to service organizations that deliver repeated services of a common kind, such as car-hire businesses, transport firms, restaurants and so on.

The alternative method is *specific order costing* sometimes called *job*, *contract* or *batch costing*. The cost unit is a particular one-off product or contract. In this case, the producer makes different but related products, which need to be costed on an individual basis. Examples of this include: making customized fitted kitchens, building a section of motorway, contract engineering or printing books.

10.6 How are costs allocated to cost centres?

In order to measure the costs against the cost centres selected, all company financial transactions are allocated a cost centre number. With modern computerized systems, this task is relatively easy, once the system has been set up.

The first step is to create a numbering system so that each cost centre has a number unique to itself. The number can be constructed in such a way that it can be used for computer sorting. Take the following sample number:

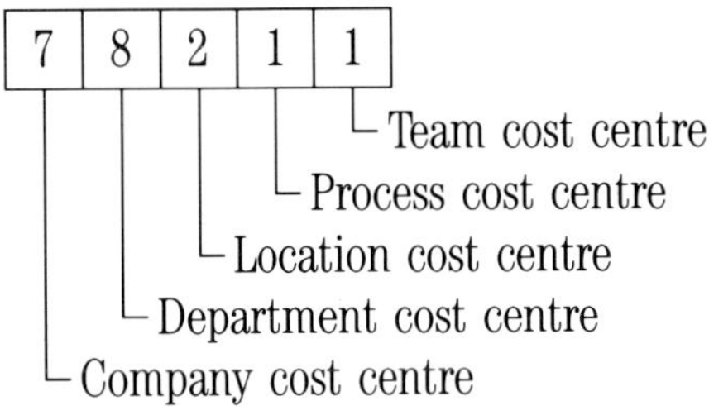

Thus, by sorting the cost centre totals as shown below, the following information can be extracted:

- All costs coded 7XXXX — total company costs
- All costs coded 78XXX — total departmental costs
- All costs coded 782XX — total costs for the particular location
- All costs coded 7821X — total process costs
- All costs coded 78211 — total costs incurred by the particular team.

In order to allocate costs to the correct cost centre, the cost centre number is recorded against each transaction. For example, each employee is allocated to a cost centre in the payroll system, so that all pay costs are charged automatically to a cost centre. Expenses forms and orders for goods and services also have to be coded with a cost centre number.

Exercise 10

In allocating managerial responsibility by department, a company has produced a series of financial and non-financial unit measures it would like to use. Which unit measure do you think would be best suited to each department? Fill in your answers in the space provided.

Department	**Unit measures**
(a) Marketing (advertising manager)	(1) Cash collected per day
(b) Manager of debt-collection	(2) Average machine down time
(c) Engineering support manager (responsible for production line maintenance)	(3) Number of enquiries outstanding at end of month
(d) Sales manager	(4) Manpower efficiency factor
(e) Administration (customer enquiries)	(5) Units produced per day
(f) Personnel manager	(6) Average cost per new recruit
(g) Flow-line production manager	(7) Sales calls per day by salesmen
(h) Work study engineer	(8) Number of sales leads per pound of advertising spent

(a) ________ (b) ________ (c) ________ (d) ________

(e) ________ (f) ________ (g) ________ (h) ________

In Exercise 10, we have tried to choose specific measures that are relevant to the departments shown. In real life, many measurements are common to a series of departments.

CHAPTER 11

Cost classification

This chapter reviews the various means by which costs are classified and explains how these classifications are used in costing systems.

11.1 Initial classification

Having allocated cost centres that reflect the perceived management information needs, we must now review the types of cost that occur and see how they match our structure.

In order to do this we must review:

- what they are
- where they occur
- how they behave
- how they can be managed.

11.2 General cost classifications

Bearing in mind the already stated requirements for management information, the general cost classifications used in a manufacturing business might be as follows:

(1) Direct production materials and components

(2) Direct production labour cost

(3) Production direct expenses

(4) Production overheads, engineering, etc.

Company overheads:

(5) Sales and marketing

(6) Distribution

(7) General administration

(8) Research and development

Prime cost = 1 + 2 + 3
Production (factory) cost = Prime cost + 4
Total cost = Production cost + 5 + 6 + 7 + 8

In non-manufacturing businesses, a similar cost structure can be built up from the main activity centres together with the overhead departments.

Exercise 11

Light Engineering Ltd, our manufacturing company, incurs a number of different types of cost, several of which are shown in the table below. You are required to analyse the costs shown in two ways:

(1) The first requirement is to allocate costs to materials, labour, and expense categories by making a mark in the appropriate column.

(2) Then using the cost classifications on page 80 (each of which is numbered between (1) and (8)), allocate a cost code classification to each cost type.

The first two lines have been completed for you as an illustration.

Cost type	*Materials*	*Labour*	*Expenses*	*Cost code*
Bought-out components	X			1
Sales commission		X		5
Materials for research				
Sheet metal for pressing				
Press operator's bonus				
TV advertisement				
Production manager's salary				
Advertisement for staff				
Office cleaning services				
Electricity for power press				
Assembly workers' overtime				
Fuel for delivery vans				
Company rates bill				
Engineering manager's salary				
Machine repair parts				
Office postage				
Research scientist's salary				
Salesman's car repairs				

11.3 How costs are classified in practice

Earlier we saw how costs are allocated to cost centres using cost centre numbers. In a similar way, expenditure is classified by type as it is incurred. In other words, as well as recording where it is incurred (or under whose authority), we also record what the cost represents.

The numbers used to classify cost types are called *nominal codes* because they are derived from the nominal ledger in bookkeeping. Originally, nominal codes were used to indicate the ledger types in which the expenditure was recorded, for example, the payroll ledger or the cash book. Nowadays, the use of computers allows much more detailed numbers to be used, thus giving more detailed classification.

If we take the case of a company using a five number code, the coding of an overtime payment could be as follows:

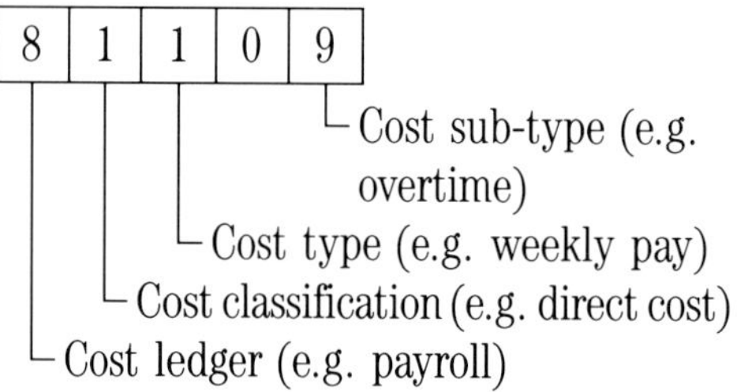

In a computerized system, costs such as this will be coded automatically by the payroll system. Other costs, such as purchases and expenses, will need to be nominal coded when they are allocated to cost centres.

Detailed cost centre and nominal coding of costs produces a database from which costs can be pinpointed very accurately. It is the system which underlies all modern computerized accounting systems.

11.4 Further classification

Having categorized costs by what they are and where they are incurred, we finally review them according to their characteristics and response to management control.

Exercise 12

Why do *you* think it is necessary to do this type of categorization? Write your answer here:

____

____

____

Now compare your answer with that given in the back of the book.

Consider the example of your personal expenditure. Some costs you have are likely to be fixed, such as rates on your house, or tax on your car, once the decision has been made to buy the assets. Other costs, such as expenditure on entertainment or on casual clothes, require a much greater element of personal decision making and are therefore far more subject to day-by-day control.

The same pattern occurs with business costs. The fixed costs of offices and factories are hard to change, but costs associated with production wastage, staff overtime, or use of office telephones for personal calls, do respond to management action. The following cost classifications are used to identify such costs:

- Direct or indirect
- Fixed or variable
- Controllable or uncontrollable.

Again, the use of these categories depends on what information the managers need. In the next pages, we will review cases in which each classification is used, starting with direct and indirect costs.

11.5 Direct and indirect costs

Once key cost areas are established, such as product types, it quickly becomes apparent that some costs can be easily attributed to a specific item or process. These are called *direct costs* and they vary according to the main activity of the business. In a manufacturing business, they would include the cost of:

- Components used directly in product manufacture
- Labour used in product manufacture.

Other costs are more difficult to allocate, usually because they apply to a number of different cost units. Examples of these include items such as factory rates, administration costs, canteen costs and so on. These are known as *indirect costs* and, as you can see, it would be difficult to allocate any of these to a specific product in a multi-product company.

To make things even more difficult, costs can be both direct *and* indirect, depending on the cost measurement and department being reviewed. A factory engineer's wages, for example, are a direct cost of the engineering department, but an indirect cost of a product.

In order to produce full product or process costings, the indirect costs have to be apportioned in some way. An engineer's cost may be apportioned by production line time taken up by each product manufactured, or in proportion to direct production labour hours. (The methods of 'absorbing' indirect costs will be dealt with in more detail when we consider absorption costing in the next chapter.)

To show how engineering costs could be allocated, using the method based on direct production hours (or alternatively on its

substitute, associated direct labour costs) we will use an example.

Company XYZ spends £1,000 per week on engineering costs, and the direct production labour costs are split as follows over the three products made:

	£
Product A	1,200
Product B	4,000
Product C	2,800
	8,000

The engineering cost by product apportioned by direct labour then becomes:

Product A =
£1,000 × 1,200/8,000 = £150
Product B =
£1,000 × 4,000/8,000 = £500
Product C =
£1,000 × 2,800/8,000 = £350

Another way of expressing this is that engineering costs represent (£1,000/£8,000 × 100) 12.5 per cent of direct labour costs, which can be applied by product. Other indirect costs apportionment methods include:

- *a percentage related to direct materials cost*. This might apply to raw materials stock costs
- *area occupied by cost centre*. This can be used for the allocation of premises costs to processes

Obviously, the method chosen must be a logical and preferably simple solution, and be used consistently.

Now complete Exercise 13 which demonstrates the use of direct and indirect costs.

Exercise 13

Use the information provided to answer the question below.

A manufacturing company has two press shops of equal area, cost centres 1 and 2. The costs incurred during the last period were as follows:

- Direct costs:
  Raw material: £20 per unit made
  Direct wages: £10 per unit made
- Indirect product costs:
  Rent and rates: £4,000
  Work study: cost centre 1: £5,000
  cost centre 2: £6,000
- Production volumes:
  Cost centre 1: 700 units
  Cost centre 2: 400 units

Complete the following cost per unit calculations:

continued

Step 1: Calculate overhead cost per unit.

	Cost centre 1	*Cost centre 2*
	£	£
Rent and rates (allocated by area £2,000 + £2,000)	2000	2000
Work study costs	5000	
Total overhead cost	7000	
Units produced	700	400
Overhead cost per unit (Total cost/units):	10	

Step 2: Calculate total cost per unit.

	Cost centre 1	*Cost centre 2*
	£	£
Direct material cost	20	
Direct labour cost	10	
Overheads (from step 1)	10	
Total cost per unit	40	

Note
This calculation does *not* mean that each unit produced by cost centre 1 costs exactly £40 to produce. This is the *average* cost per unit.

11.6 Fixed and variable costs

Another important way of considering costs is in terms of *fixed* and *variable* costs. When we allocate these costs, we do so according to their behaviour when the business volume alters. Fixed costs are those costs which stay constant, no matter what volume of business the company achieves. Variable costs, as their name implies, vary with the volume of throughput or activity.

Let us take the example of a distribution department in a manufacturing company. The fixed costs will be incurred whether any product is moved or not and might include:

- distribution depot premises costs — rent, rates and so on

- some labour costs — the distribution manager
- some vehicle costs — vehicle taxation and insurance.

These costs would be incurred whether we moved 1 unit or 10,000 units.

Costs which vary with the amount of units delivered include:

- packing costs
- some labour cost — cost of drivers
- variable vehicle costs — fuel and maintenance.

Another way of displaying the impact of fixed and variable costs is by a graph. Taking some sample figures for our distribution department, we can produce the graph shown below.

Figure 4: Distribution department — fixed and variable costs

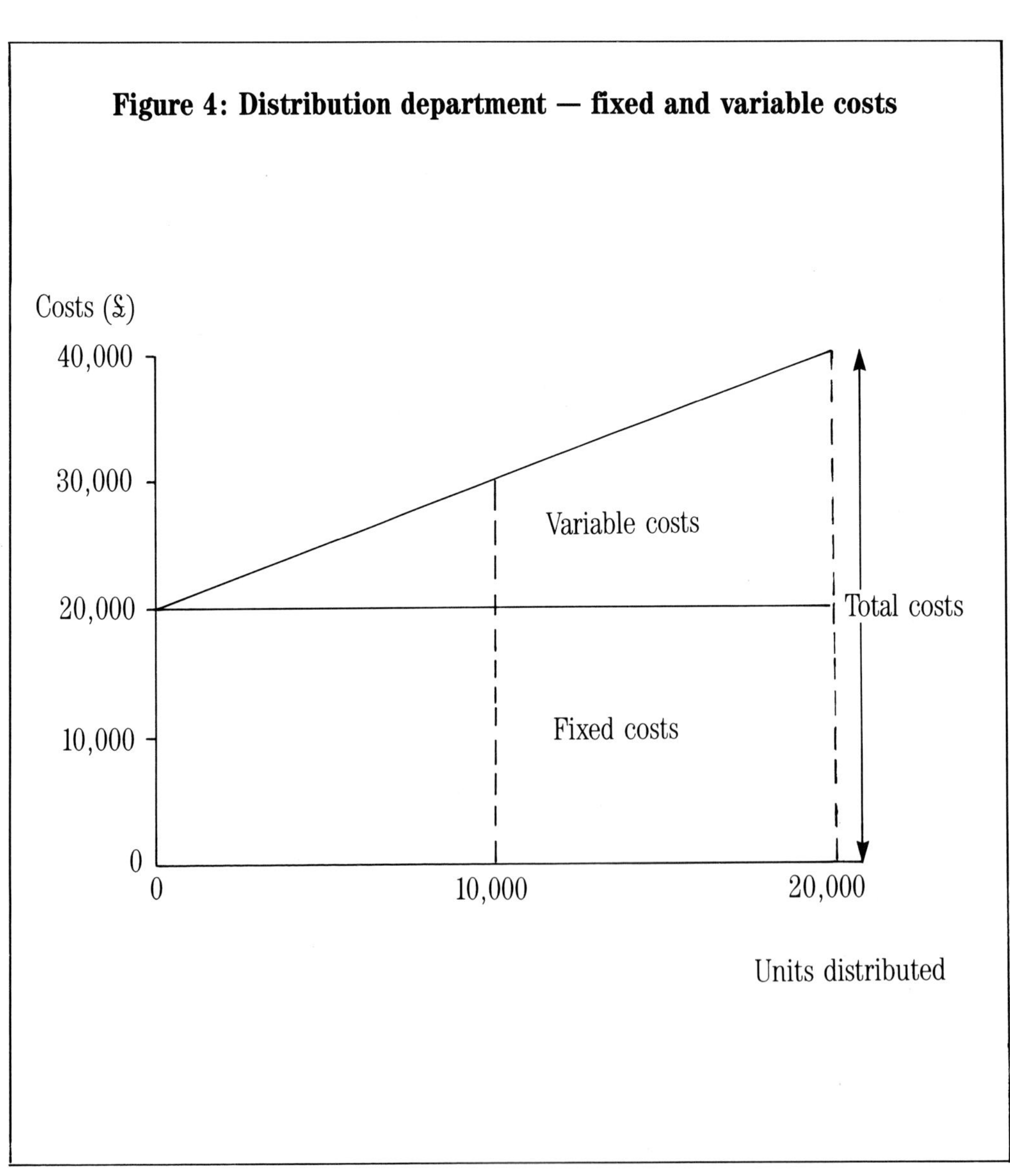

Using the graph we can see that the total distribution cost, and hence the cost per unit (at different volumes) is as follows:

- To distribute 1 unit:

	Total cost £	*Cost per unit* £
Fixed costs	20,000	20,000
Variable costs	1	1
Total	20,001	20,001

- To distribute 1000 units:

	Total cost £	*Cost per unit* £
Fixed costs	20,000	2
Variable costs	10,000	1
Total	30,000	3

- To distribute 20,000 units:

	Total cost £	*Cost per unit* £
Fixed costs	20,000	1
Variable costs	20,000	1
Total	40,000	2

It is unlikely that only one unit would be distributed, but, if it were, that one unit would cost the department £20,001 to deliver! More realistically, we can see the effect of achieving increased volumes, from 10,000 units to 20,000 units, which produces a reduction in unit distribution cost from £3 to £2.

You should see from this example the effect of increasing volume of throughput, or activity, on fixed costs per unit. Whatever department we work in, the higher the volume, the lower the unit price (up to maximum capacity, of course).

For advantages like these, companies seek to attain higher volumes through fixed cost locations. One example is the introduction of double shift working as opposed to setting up an additional single shift line. Of course, this type of action produces other benefits as well, such as better use of capital investment.

The one problem with this type of cost categorization is that, in reality, few costs are either totally fixed or directly variable with changes in volume. For example, in a distribution department, drivers cannot be hired and laid off day by day according to the numbers of units to be delivered. They are not, therefore, directly variable with activity. Similarly, fixed costs are only fixed up to a point. Efficient distribution operations hold a core of permanent staff and vehicles sufficient to cope with normal daily distribution needs. Activity peaks are then dealt with using contract hire.

This means, in practice, that many costs are *semi-variable*, that is, they do vary with volume, but not directly. The term 'semi-variable' is often used to describe support costs. For example, in a large distribution operation there might be one records clerk to every ten warehouse storeman. As volume increases storemen would be added on a direct basis to cope with the increased volume. Additional records clerks would only be added as necessary.

Although these costs may not behave perfectly, it does not lessen the importance of understanding the nature of costs in improving company efficiency. Because of this imperfect behaviour of costs, graphs showing the actual movement of costs with units sold, produced, delivered etc. may look more like the graph shown overleaf.

Figure 5: Movement of costs with activity

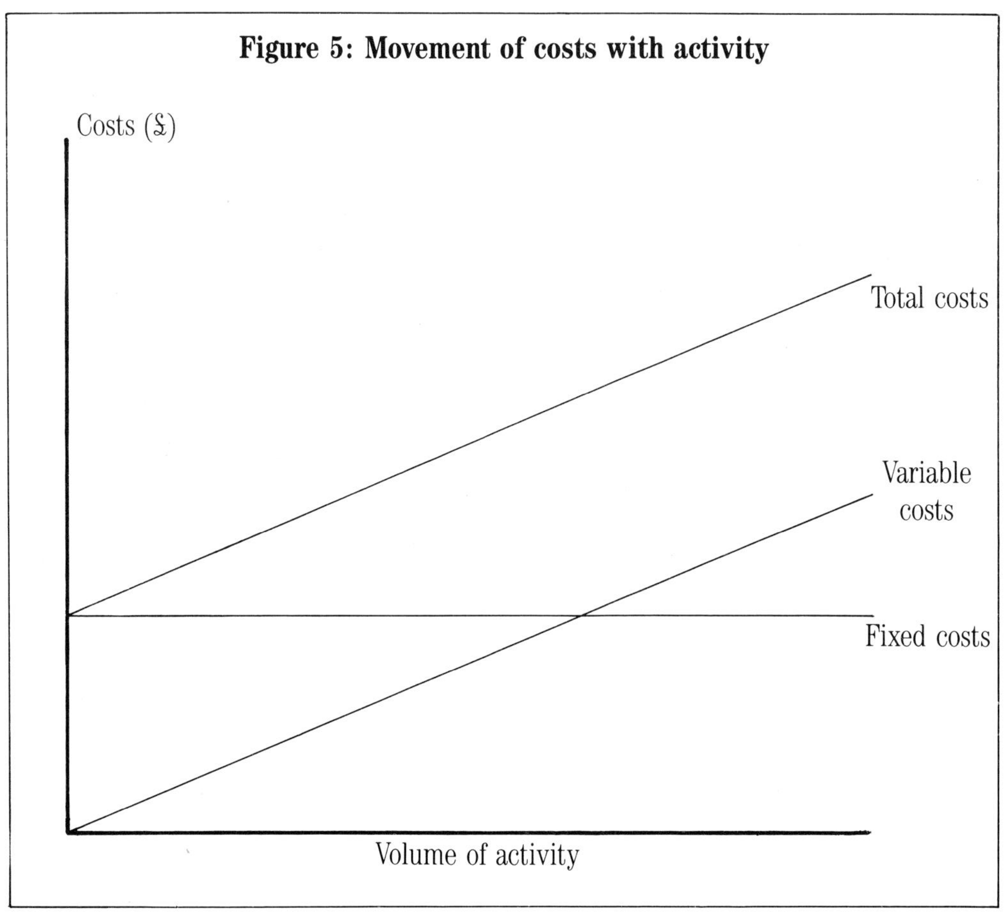

Now, to check your understanding of fixed and variable costs do exercise 14.

Exercise 14

Categorize the following production costs as fixed (F), variable (V), or semi-variable (SV) according to their relationship with the volume of product manufactured.

(a) The factory manager's salary ____

(b) Component costs (constant per unit made) ____

(c) Quality checkers (1 per line up to 5,000 units produced, 2 over 5,000)

continued

(d) Electricity costs (£x per production unit throughput) ____

(e) Factory personnel department costs ____

(f) Plant maintenance costs (standard per 1,000 hours of operation) ____

(g) Royalty costs — the company pays a fixed fee of £100 for the first 500 produced, and then 5p per unit. ____

11.7 Controllable and uncontrollable costs

The final cost categorization to consider is based on measuring the ability of a manager to influence particular costs within his budget responsibility.

Controllable costs are those over which a manager has control and can therefore change. *Uncontrollable* costs are those within his overall budget responsibility but which he cannot change. For example, if the estates manager of a company is involved in discussions which lead to a 50 per cent increase in the annual factory rent, the production manager can hardly be made accountable for this increase.

If we inspect the costs incurred within a department, we can review each cost item for controllability. Take, for example, the annual costs of an accounts department as given below.

Annual costs of an accounts department

	Annual costs £
Wages, salaries and benefits	50,000
Overtime at year-end for accounts	2,000
Temporary staff for stocktaking	3,000
Stationery and office supplies	5,000
Postage and telephones	6,000
Computer recharges (based on usage)	15,000
Other allocated costs:	
Rent and rates	2,500
Heat, light, cleaning etc.	3,000
Other central charges	2,500
Total	89,000

How controllable are these costs in practice? Take each line in turn and draw your own conclusions before going on to the next paragraph.

The manpower costs are related to the number of people employed (which in turn is determined by the amount of work to be done at current staff productivity or efficiency levels), and the cost per person. These costs are only partially controllable as the number of people employed is likely to be flexible only to a small degree. Similarly, the pay rates for each individual are likely to be determined by national negotiations and outside the power of a local manager. The controllable manpower costs are the management of overtime and the use of temporary staff.

Some of the cost categories are more easily controlled than others: telephone costs, for example, are notoriously hard to control in offices where outside access is generally necessary. Other cost categories will require control involving 'trade-off' decisions. For example, it may well be possible to trade off manpower costs against computer costs. In other words, computer services should replace existing manual tasks.

As we saw before, the allocated costs are likely to be largely uncontrollable.

Again, the two categories do not always exist in a perfect state. The classification of a particular cost as controllable may well be done when senior managers wish to place general emphasis on the item. For example, a drive to reduce telephone costs may be initiated by declaring telephone costs a major controllable item. The importance of this classification is that it is used to highlight responsibilities and accountabilities. *All* costs are 'controllable' by *somebody*, and it is important that that individual is held responsible. However, it is also necessary to show uncontrollable costs allocated by department, or product, so that total costs may be appreciated. In this way, managers, whilst having overall responsibility for total departmental costs, can be measured specifically against controllable cost items.

The types of cost classification reviewed in this chapter have value in the particular circumstances described. Each is therefore applied to highlight particular cost groupings. In this way, management attention can be focused on items of significance in the cost structure of the company.

CHAPTER 12

Costing techniques

This chapter reviews the main costing techniques used in industry and commerce.

We have now examined many of the elements used in designing costing systems, but we now need to examine how these come together as operational techniques. These techniques include:

- standard costing
- absorption costing
- marginal costing.

Each of these is valuable in particular situations, so, in addition to describing the technique itself, we will investigate the practical uses of each one.

12.1 Standard costing

This technique, which is the most widely used costing method, is based upon setting *standards* for each activity or process. The standards agreed should represent *normal, efficient performance*. This is an extremely important point, as they should be clearly distinguished from targets or goals, which are performances that *could be achieved*, given optimum conditions.

There are many benefits arising from the introduction of standard costing. These include:

- the establishment of detailed measures of expected performance down to the lowest level in the organization
- provision of a framework on which to hang many non-financial measures — for example manpower performance statistics (work study), machine and equipment performance
- a standard product costing format that can be used for product comparison, cost reduction programmes and as a basis for stock and work-in-progress evaluation
- the production of a consistent costing methodology on which to build management decisions:
  - ★ pricing decisions
  - ★ make-or-buy decisions
  - ★ decisions on factory loadings/capacities
- the creation of a base on which to build future plans, a topic we will deal with in more detail in a later chapter.

12.2 Compilation of a standard product or process cost

Standard costs are usually based on experience. Of course, if a new product, service or process is to be carried out, the initial standard costs will have to be estimated and, as more knowledge is acquired about actual costs, the standards can be updated and refined.

Each business must have a definition of what it means by standard cost. A typical definition of a standard cost of a product might be as follows:

The standard cost of a product represents the expenditure allowed on direct material, direct wages and production overheads required to produce goods at the required quality and design when operating at a standard level of activity, with proven methods and with current material prices and labour rates.

Where high volume products or services are involved, quite small variations in standard cost may cause significant changes in overall business profitability. Great care is therefore needed to ensure that the standard costs are realistic and accurate. A company such as Mars, for instance, may be producing over one million units a week. Small changes in unit standard costs will be repeated some 50 million times in a year.

The following is an example of how a standard product cost of a car battery could be produced:

Product specification — battery no. 101

Material/component	*Quantity per battery*	*Cost per battery (pence per battery)* Material	*Labour*	*O'head*	*Total*	*Std time /100*
Container	1	60	2	nil	62	25
Lid	1	35	nil	nil	35	nil
Positive plates	20	75	15	90	180	180
Negative plates	20	75	12	75	162	150
Separators	34	30	nil	nil	30	nil
Manifold	1	30	nil	nil	30	nil
Battery assembly	1	10	65	150	225	850
Charging	1	20	30	90	140	450
		335	124	405	864	1655

The standard cost is therefore 864 pence or $8.64 per battery.

Notes on the battery costing:

(1) The items with no labour cost are purchased components.

(2) Underlying this table are a number of sub-specifications and calculations including:

(a) *Material specifications*
Design drawings
Process capability — losses/wastage
Buying — bought-out cost of components
Material commodity prices — lead, copper

(b) *Labour*
Standard times (work study)
Machine speeds, gang sizes, grades

(c) *Overheads*
Rate per cost centre
Overall allocation.

12.3 Absorption costing

Absorption costing is a technique by which the overheads and indirect costs associated with a product, contract or service are allocated to that unit. In other words, it is the way in which costs are absorbed by the unit. This technique is not a complete costing method and can, for instance, form part of a standard costing system.

Overheads don't need to be absorbed in every circumstance as we will discover in the next section on marginal costing. However, if we require a *full* costing of a particular product — for example, when we wish to set prices, we will need to know the total costs connected with that product.

We have already seen some examples of overhead cost allocation earlier in this module. What we need to consider now is the choice of method to be used.

In most cases, we should know the total overhead cost by type as incurred by the company, and therefore need to distribute the cost by product or contract unit. In order to approach this task logically, it is necessary to identify the major factors causing the overhead to be incurred so we can attribute overheads against these factors. For example, in Chapter 10 we used an example in which premises costs were allocated according to factory space occupied, space occupied being the major factor in determining premises costs.

In setting a basis for the allocation or absorption of overheads, we must be aware of the need to produce a simple, practical method. In other words, a method which involves the use of complex data, or information which is difficult to obtain, should be avoided.

Now let us see how manufacturing overheads may be dealt with.

Manufacturing overheads

When considering the absorption of manufacturing overheads, attention should be paid to the major factors affecting overheads which are:

- direct materials (their management, handling and control)
- direct labour (all the overheads driven by employment)
- direct expenses.

These factors are produced as a matter of course in a product or process costing. Any or all of these factors may be used as a basis for overhead costs. Direct labour, for instance, is commonly used as a basis for allocating total overhead costs, because it reflects the time spent in production. That is, the longer the time spent in production, the higher the direct labour charge, and the greater the overheads incurred. This method has additional advantages in that labour rates are fairly constant (compared with material content), and the associated overhead costs are closely connected with manpower numbers.

To demonstrate the use of this method, let us consider an example.

Example

A manufacturing company producing a wide range of products has the following annual production costs:

	Cost
	£'000
Direct materials	560
Direct labour	850
Direct expenses	150
Prime cost	1560
Total overhead	640
Works cost	2200

It has been decided that as overhead costs are closely related to direct labour, product costings will absorb overhead on a direct labour cost basis. We now have to complete the following product costings based on this method. To do so, we have to calculate the absorption factor. This is done by establishing the relationship between total overhead and total direct labour, using the following equation:

Total overhead =

$$\frac{640}{850} \times \frac{100}{1} = 75 \text{ per cent of direct labour}$$

This can now be used in product unit costings:

	Product 1	*Product 2*
Known direct product costs:	£	£
Materials	5	5
Labour	8	9
Expenses	2	1
Prime cost	15	15
Works overhead (75 per cent × labour)	6	6.75
Works cost	21	21.75

In other situations, direct materials cost or prime cost can be used as a base if it is considered that they better indicate overhead spent. Similarly, in more detailed costings, costs may be allocated more specifically, using, for example, factors such as machine hours worked, or direct labour hours worked.

Other overheads

Once manufacturing overheads have been absorbed, the remaining company overheads can be applied.

Selling, distribution and other costs usually comprise a mixture of direct and indirect costs. Some cost items such as an advertising campaign for a specific product may be directly allocated, whilst others may be much more general and difficult to attribute, for example, a general company advertising campaign. The non-specific costs may be absorbed in one of three ways:

(1) rate per item

(2) percentage on selling price

(3) percentage on work cost.

(1) Rate per item

In this method all overhead costs are allocated to product items in the best way available to us. Each cost is considered separately and allocated in the best way. Fixed costs, such as that of a sales showroom, may be allocated by product turnover or volumes. Variable costs can then be allocated on a per item basis. The way in which this is performed is shown in the example below.

Example: Company XYZ
Absorption of selling and distribution costs

	Products		
	1	*2*	*3*
Fixed costs (allocated in total)	£5,000	£44,000	£20,000
Sales units	10,000	100,000	50,000
Cost per unit	£0.5	£0.44	£0.4
Unit costs (rate per item)	£	£	£
Fixed costs per unit (as above	0.5	0.44	0.4
Variable costs:			
Commission	0.4	0.3	0.3
Packing	0.3	0.3	0.3
Freight	0.3	0.2	0.3
Sales and distribution cost per unit	1.5	1.24	1.3

These allocations can then be added to the manufacturing cost per unit.

(2) Percentage on selling price
The percentage on selling price method of absorbing costs is often used when sales are made through different distribution channels, which represent the various ways of selling, for example, by using a salesforce to sell directly to the public, or by using a retail store chain, or distributors.

Dealers or agents are likely to work on a discount or commission basis, with the payment being related to sales turnover. Selling and distribution is therefore delegated to these third parties on that basis.

The percentage on selling price is also used in calculating the 'ideal' ex-works cost. In other words, by taking a competitive market price of a product, we can work back to produce a target manufacturing cost consistent with that sales price. If we use the example of a company selling typewriters, we find that they are selling through their own salesforce, through a national distributor, and through local dealers.

The next example shows how the selling and distribution costs and the discount given appear when considered as a percentage of the product list price.

Example: AB Typewriters
Selling and distribution costs

	National distributor	*Dealer*	*Own sales force*
	%	%	%
List price	100	100	100
Discount (average)	45	35	10
Actual sales income	55	65	90
Sales and distribution cost	10	20	45
Ex-works cost and profit	45	45	45

Note
The price we have used is the 'list price'. This is a price which is in fact seldom charged — even the company's own salesforce give an average of 10 per cent discount. Nevertheless, it is a price which is published and therefore a good base.

As you can see this typewriter company has to manufacture its product at a cost (including profit) total 45 per cent less than the published list price.

(3) Percentage on manufacturing cost
This final method is used when products are similar and/or of similar value. For instance, the battery costing example shown earlier in this chapter (p. 93) produced a production cost per battery of £8.64. To make that up to a full product cost, we need to add in the remaining cost items, which are administration, selling and distribution. The way in which this can be done is shown below.

Battery unit cost

	£
Standard cost (as calculated previously)	8.64
Distribution (£1 per item)	1.00
Administration and selling (At 10% of standard cost)	0.86
	10.50

Note that the 10 per cent of administration and selling has been added on a cost plus basis, using the normal company percentage.

12.4 Marginal costing

In the previous section we saw how the allocation of fixed and overhead costs involves the widespread use of assumptions. This can be both complex and difficult to administer, but it is a necessary part of producing total costings.

In many cases, we do not need to calculate the total cost but rather measure relative effects such as:

- the effect of changing production or sales volume, or
- the relative benefits of individual products.

To perform this we can use *marginal costing*, which is a technique for relative measurement rather than total cost measurement.

A strict definition of marginal cost is:

The change in cost which occurs when the volume of output is increased or reduced by one unit.

In practice, this is measured by the total variable cost for one unit. Marginal costing is therefore dependent on being able to identify and separate fixed and variable costs (as reviewed in the previous chapter). Taking a single-product company as an example, the following costs have been recorded for a recent period, together with the analysis into fixed and variable elements.

Company cost analysis

	Total	*Fixed*	*Variable*
	£	£	£
Sales (40,000 units)	20,000		
Costs			
Direct materials	4,000	nil	4,000
Direct labour	4,000	2,000	2,000
Production overhead	2,000	2,000	nil
Sales and marketing	3,500	2,000	1,500
Distribution	2,500	1,500	1,000
Research and development	1,000	1,000	nil
General administration	1,000	1,000	nil
Total costs	18,000	9,500	8,500
Net profit	2,000		

To display these costs on a marginal basis we can rearrange the figures as follows.

Marginal costing

		Unit basis
	£	£
Sales	20,000	0.5
Less: Variable costs	8,500	0.21
Contribution*	11,500	0.29
Less: Fixed costs	9,500	0.24
Net profit	2,000	0.05

From this we can deduce that for every one unit increase in sales we produce a revenue of £0.5 (50p) and a contribution of £0.29 (29p). As fixed costs will not change, the contribution represents additional profit. Profit on a marginal basis is therefore 29p per unit compared with 5p per unit for the base 40,000 units.

If we increase sales by 10 per cent, sales variable costs and contribution will all increase by 10 per cent (contribution increases by £1,150). Profit however will also increase by £1,150 because the fixed costs do not change — an increase of 57.5 per cent. This sensitivity of profit to volume is important for companies to manage. As in the previous section on fixed and variable costs, it is best portrayed using a graph. The graph shown overleaf is a *break-even* graph, produced by adding the revenue growth line to the fixed and variable cost totals. The break-even point is that in which the volume is sufficient to make sales income match costs. Below this volume, the company will operate at a loss, above it, it will make an increasing profit.

The graph shown uses the figures developed above.

*The result of deducting variable costs from sales income is known as 'contribution'. This is an abbreviation of contribution towards fixed costs and profit.

Figure 6: Break-even graph

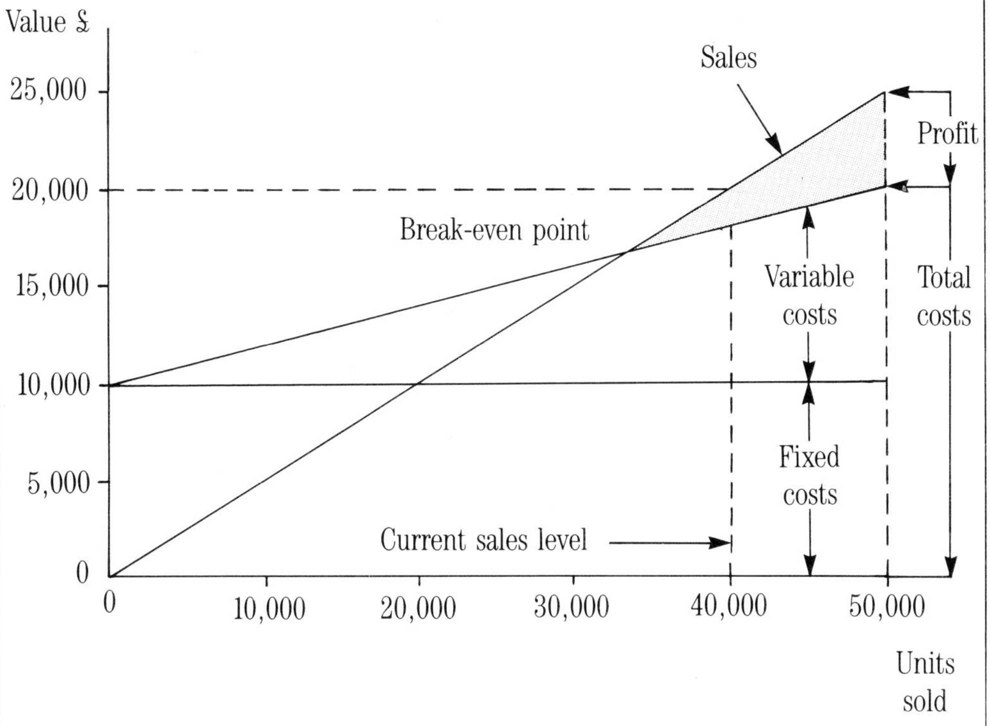

12.5 The costing process schematic diagram

This chapter can best be reviewed by reference to a flow chart of costing. This flow chart, shown below, summarizes the overall costing process and shows how the techniques and methods are connected. In particular, you should note the inter-relationships between the various costing elements discussed. As you can see, the costing process flows through the whole business to provide managers with a database upon which major decisions can be made. It also provides managers with a 'history book' — a record of costs by product, process, department or whatever parameter is selected as a key measure.

Figure 7: Flow chart of costing techniques and methods

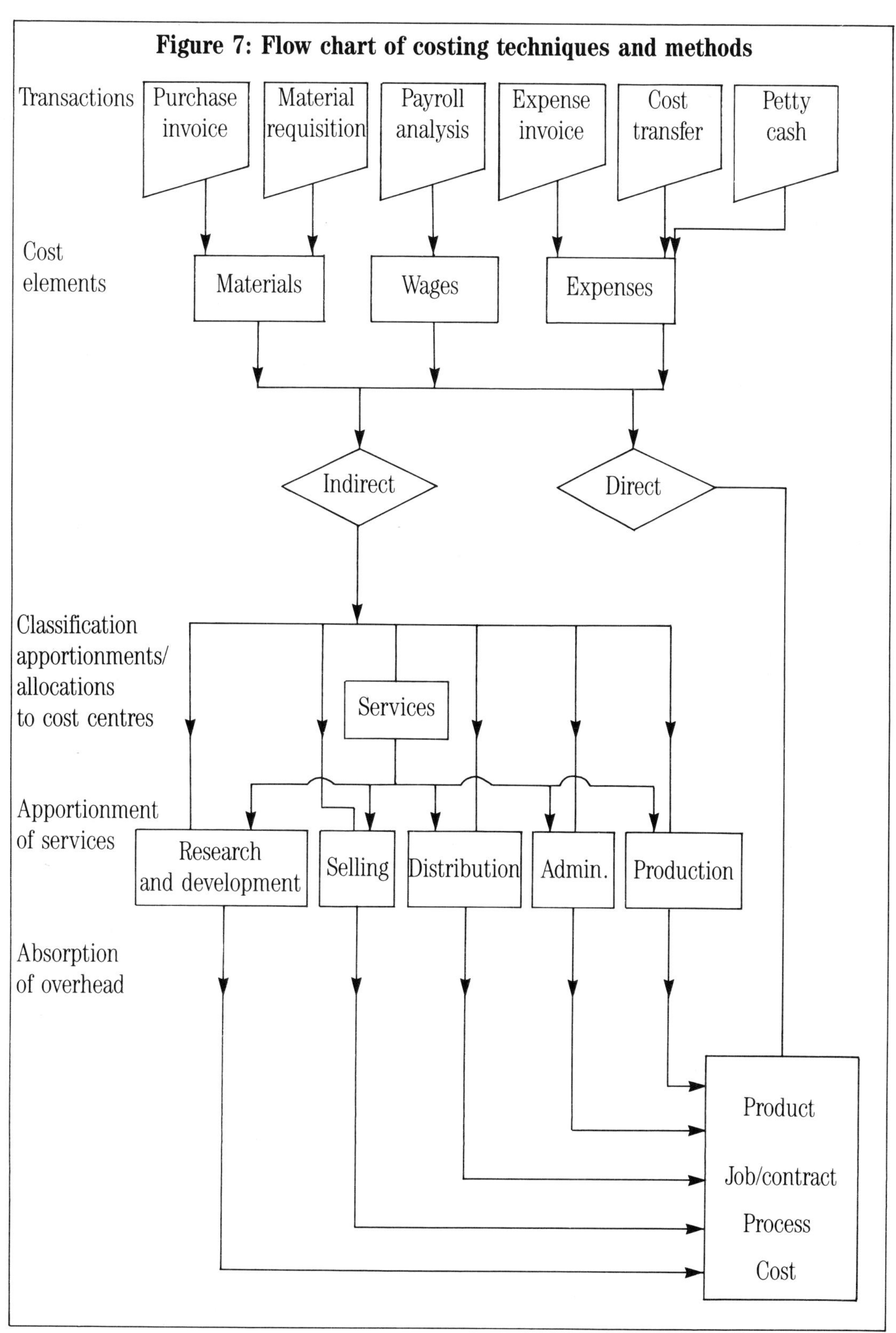

CHAPTER 13

Profit and loss management issues

This chapter shows some ways in which costing techniques are used in financial analysis, thereby facilitating management decision making.

Previous chapters have provided you with an understanding of the structure and techniques of cost accounting. It is now time to see how cost accounting is used to support some of the key management decisions affecting business profitability. The decision areas covered are:

- pricing
- make-or-buy decisions
- adding or deleting products.

13.1 Pricing

For most companies business is highly competitive — if your company's products do not satisfy your customer's needs in terms of quality, performance, delivery time, or price, he will go elsewhere.

Pricing will clearly be a dominant factor in influencing sales in many markets. However, it is important to remember that maintaining a low price is not the only factor to be considered — value for money is what the customer is normally seeking. For instance, the owner of a Rolls Royce may well believe that he is getting value for money but he is certainly not buying the cheapest product on the market.

Having said that, the setting of prices is an extremely important management function. Three prime considerations have to be taken into account in making pricing decisions:

- what the customer is prepared to pay for the product
- the cost of making, selling and delivering the product
- the level of profit required by the selling company.

Many companies have traditionally priced their product on *cost-plus* basis (total cost plus profit). They could do this because they were dominant suppliers in their market place and could more or less charge whatever they wanted. However, nowadays, increased competitive pressures have led to prices being much more market (i.e. consumer) driven.

But pricing, whatever method you use, is not always a simple process. For example, the unit cost of a product can vary with the volume produced. Alternatively, in multi-product factories, it may be difficult to allocate fixed costs and overheads to particular products.

The usual way of working out *mark-up* or *cost-plus* prices is to take the manufacturing costs of a product and add a fixed percentage to produce a selling price (a technique first shown in the section on absorption costing in Chapter 12). This percentage covers all the costs that are not easily attributable to specific products — selling, administration and other central overheads — and, in addition, allows an appropriate profit to be made. This method has to be based on experience and past costing records in order to produce a reasonable profit result.

The attainment of a good result is compounded by the fact that the price of the product will have an effect on the volume of sales achieved. In turn, the volume of sales will have an impact on unit costs as the fixed costs are distributed over differing unit volumes.

This can be illustrated in numerical terms by using an example. We have chosen a company which uses a standard mark-up of 40 per cent on factory transfer price. This mark-up covers administration and selling costs plus a suitable profit margin. The product featured can be sold in volumes varying between 50,000 and 150,000 units, according to price set. The cost calculation demonstrating how the price charged can vary with volume is shown below.

Example: Calculation of price by the mark-up method

Units	*50k*	*100k*	*150k*
Cost per unit	£	£	£
Direct materials	4.5	4.5	4.5
Direct labour	3.0	3.0	3.0
Variable overheads	2.0	2.0	2.0
Fixed overheads	3.0	1.5	1.0
Factory cost	12.5	11.0	10.5
Mark-up (40%)	5.0	4.4	4.2
Selling price	17.5	15.4	14.7

As you can see from the example, the difference in unit cost resulting from the absorption of fixed overheads over differing volumes, causes considerable variation in the possible selling prices.

From this type of data, company management must select the optimum price/volume balance. In some cases, company policy will determine the choice. Rolls Royce Motors have already been quoted as an example of a high price/low volume company. For 'discount' stores, such as Comet, a low price/high volume policy is preferred. The choice of policy does not matter as long as the price and volume options match, and the other features of the product are consistent with the policy — they reinforce the customer's view in terms of apparent value for money.

Finally, further pricing options occur once sufficient volume has been sold at a price that covers fixed overheads. At this stage, the product can be sold on a *marginal cost* basis. In other words, the price charged can be the variable costs plus a profit margin. It is quite common for excess volumes to be disposed of in such a way.

It cannot be stressed too strongly that the achievement of sales volumes that cover fixed costs is an important priority for all companies (and company profit centres). Once such volumes have been secured, the company can be far more flexible in its marketing approach.

13.2 Make-or-buy decisions

In managing a manufacturing business, it is often necessary to decide between buying components from suppliers or manufacturing them yourself. There are many other business decisions which involve a choice between performing a service yourself or hiring another company to do it. For example, you may wish to operate your own transport fleet, alternatively you may use a sub-contractor.

This decision can be made in terms of:

- increased profit
- non-financial factors (available skills, etc.)
- the adequacy of the return on any investment required.

Note that it is the *incremental* cost or profit that is measured. In other words, we use marginal costing, as described in Chapter 12.

Example

A company currently buys out 50,000 of a component part per year at a cost of £1.50 each. The possibility of manufacturing the part internally is being considered. The part costings show that direct costs of manufacturing would be:

Direct materials	£0.5 per unit
Direct labour	£0.5 per unit

The department overhead rate is 100 per cent on direct costs. Estimated additional departmental costs incurred would be:

Extra management	£2,500
Additional services	£2,000
Extra maintenance	£4,000
Extra depreciation	£1,500
Other expenses	£1,000

Comparison of costs

Bought out		*Manufactured*	
50,000 at £1.50:	£75,000	*Direct costs*	
		50,000 at £1	£50,000
		Additional overheads (as above)	£11,000
			£61,000

By comparing the alternatives, we can see that the company would save:

£75,000 – £61,000 = £14,000

per year by manufacturing the part.

Note that only incremental costs are included. Overheads, apart from those specifically mentioned, do not change. The general overhead percentage is therefore not applied.

The company will have to consider the non-financial implications, as well as the return on investment, which we review later.

13.3 Adding or deleting products or services

The question of product-line profitability is the last element we will review here. Again, it is a commonly encountered problem, with more complex implications than are first apparent. For this reason, while a product or service may *appear* to be making an overall loss, dropping the product may have a serious effect on profitability, because the fixed costs and overheads now have to be absorbed by a smaller base.

To demonstrate this, if we have a company making several products, we can assess the profitability of each product on an individual basis, as shown in the example below.

Product review

Product	*A*	*B*	*C*	*D*	*E*
	£	£	£	£	£
Price	33.0	16.5	14.0	22.0	18.0
Materials	10.0	5.0	4.0	9.0	6.5
Labour	8.0	4.0	3.6	6.0	4.0
Overheads (150% labour)	12.0	6.0	5.4	9.0	6.0
Total cost	30.0	15.0	13.0	24.0	16.5
Profit	3.0	1.5	1.0	(2.0)	1.5
Sales volume (K = '000)	5K	18K	17K	14K	10K

At first sight, the obvious course of action appears to be to drop product D — the loss-making product — thereby apparently saving (14K × £2.0) £28,000. However, 50 per cent of the overheads are fixed, and would still occur. The actual loss eliminated would therefore be:

Loss of revenue 14,000 × £22.0		£308,000
Costs saved		
Materials	14,000 × £9.0	£126,000
Labour	14,000 × £6.0	£ 84,000
Overheads	14,000 × £9.0 × 50%	£ 63,000
		£273,000
Net effect: *Reduction in profit*		£ 35,000

Therefore eliminating the 'loss-making' product would actually worsen overall profits.

Once again, factors other than financial ones have to be considered in making decisions. However, you can begin to appreciate how a reduction in product lines can begin a downward profit spiral as overheads are spread over fewer and fewer products, each then becoming unprofitable in turn.

It has become apparent in recent years that expansion is far easier to manage in business than contraction. In other words, profit improvement through business growth is much easier to manage than profit improvement produced by managing a gradual decline — through reducing costs at a faster rate than revenue is falling. For this reason, management should always be aware of the need to improve existing products and develop new lines and market-places. In this way, the company can take the best advantage of the opportunities presented to it and stay competitive and profitable.

PART 3

Planning and budgeting

CHAPTER 14

Planning and budgeting

This chapter introduces the important topics of *planning*, *forecasting* and *budgeting*. Each is defined and its role in management reviewed.

14.1 An introduction to planning and budgeting

We have now examined in some detail the way in which costs are measured and controlled. You should now understand the process and techniques by which costs are recorded and reported. However, as you probably realized, so far the book has concentrated on the reporting and control aspects of finance — past and present events. It is now time that we moved on to the future. An important role of management is planning for the future and implementing the decisions that will sustain and improve company profitability. This can be seen in the figure below, which portrays, in simple terms, the process of management and the way in which the finance roles match the process.

Figure 8: The management process

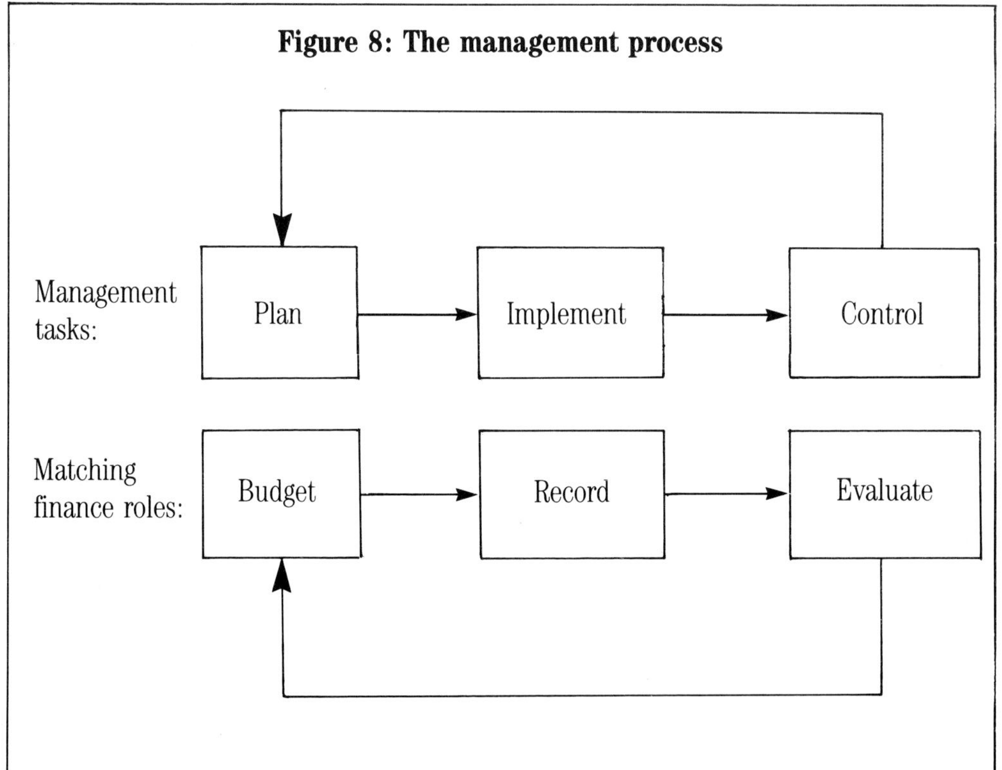

As you can see, knowledge of past and present events form the basis of determining future policy. In this way, management can lead business development positively rather than merely being a follower of others.

The management process shown in figure 8 above covers virtually all management decisions. For example, think of management decisions (or even personal decisions) you have been involved in and consider how knowledge of past events was used in planning and implementing decisions concerning the future. In the following chapters you will learn how plans and budgets are prepared, and how they are used in managing the business.

14.2 What is a budget?

At the same time as defining the term *budget* it is important to clarify the meaning of *forecasts* and *plans*. These terms are often used interchangeably in practice, but they do have different meanings.

First of all how would you define each term? Write your own definition below:

A *budget* is ______________________

____

A *forecast* is______________________

____

A *plan* is______________________

____

Now read the following text and see how your version compares with the definitions given.

The role of *planning* is to create approved future policies for a company over a given period of time. The purpose of these policies is to enable the company to achieve its objectives. Plans do not have to be expressed in financial terms, for example, a personnel department may develop plans in terms of employee conditions or recruitment policies.

A *budget* is a plan expressed in financial terms. Budgets can vary in size from a personal budget developed for an individual, to the total annual budget produced by the government for the whole country.

The difference between a *forecast* and a budget is that a forecast is a prediction of what will happen in a particular situation — it can be a judgement by any competent person — whereas a budget is a target that a business aims to achieve. Moreover, when approved and issued, a budget is a directive to employees to work to achieve the business objectives.

Budgeting relies on the basic control factors used in cost accounting, as these form the major measures to be influenced when managing and controlling the business in the future.

A more precise definition of a budget might therefore be:

A financial or quantitative statement, prepared in advance of a period of time, reflecting the agreed policies and strategies necessary to meet objectives.

We should all be familiar with the idea of a budget. Few of us embark on any large personal spending project without estimating what it will cost — even if we don't write it down. If, for instance, we are planning to take a holiday, we are likely to spend some time considering where, when, and how we are going to go. Included in this will be an estimate of what it is likely to cost us, so that we can arrange the appropriate funding. Furthermore, if half way through the holiday we find that we have spent more than we planned, we may have to alter our spending pattern to stay within our total limit. Or alternatively, make arrangements for extra money to be available! Company budgetary control follows along very much the same lines, the main steps of the process being:

(1) Definition of objectives

(2) Allocation of responsibilities for achievement of objectives

(3) Statement of policies and strategies necessary to achieve the objectives

(4) Budget preparation — calculation of likely results

(5) Budget approval

(6) Implementation of policies and strategies

(7) Measurement of progress — actual performance versus budget

(8) Revision of policy to reflect actual conditions and new circumstances.

Before going into the process of preparing budgets, it is worth spending a little time considering how the whole planning and budgeting process fits into a company structure.

14.3 The planning process

There are several different approaches a company can use in planning for the future. The approaches are normally distinguished by the length of time covered, and can therefore be categorized as:

- Long-term plans
- Medium-term plans
- Short-term plans.

So, what is meant by these terms?

There is no universal definition of the time-span covered by each of these categories. However, the long- and medium-term plans may be known as *corporate* or *strategic* plans. The use of such plans depends on a number of factors including:

- The type of business
- The markets served by the business
- The need for decisions regarding future events and products
- The importance placed by management on planning as a management tool.

The purpose of each type of process is as follows:

Long-term planning is an exercise aimed at assessing future socio-economic and business trends for periods of up to twenty years. It is important to be aware of these trends in order to determine strategies which will sustain company growth and meet corporate objectives in the long term.

Long-term planning assumes a more specific role in areas such as the aerospace industry, where product lead times may be as long as five to ten years. It is important to assess whether the market will still exist when the product finally emerges. However, in the micro-computer software industry, the rate of change is so rapid that long-term plans are likely to add little benefit to management decision making.

Medium-term planning is a more practical exercise and normally has a time horizon of two to five years. It is more practical because the closer we are to the present day, the fewer assumptions have to be made, and the probability of the plan reflecting what actually happens is much greater.

The medium-term plan will reflect the outline strategies developed in the long-term plan, but concentrate on the major decisions necessary in the next two to five years. These decisions will include areas such as: product life cycles (the need for new and replacement products), utilization of premises, development of manpower and so on.

Short-term planning or budgeting normally covers a period of a year, and, unlike the others, may be subject to revision within that year. Because it deals with the immediate future, it is subject to much more certainty and can provide a detailed statement of intent. Short-term plans are therefore produced in much more detail than the others.

The relationship between the planning processes is shown in detail overleaf.

Figure 9: The relationship between the planning processes

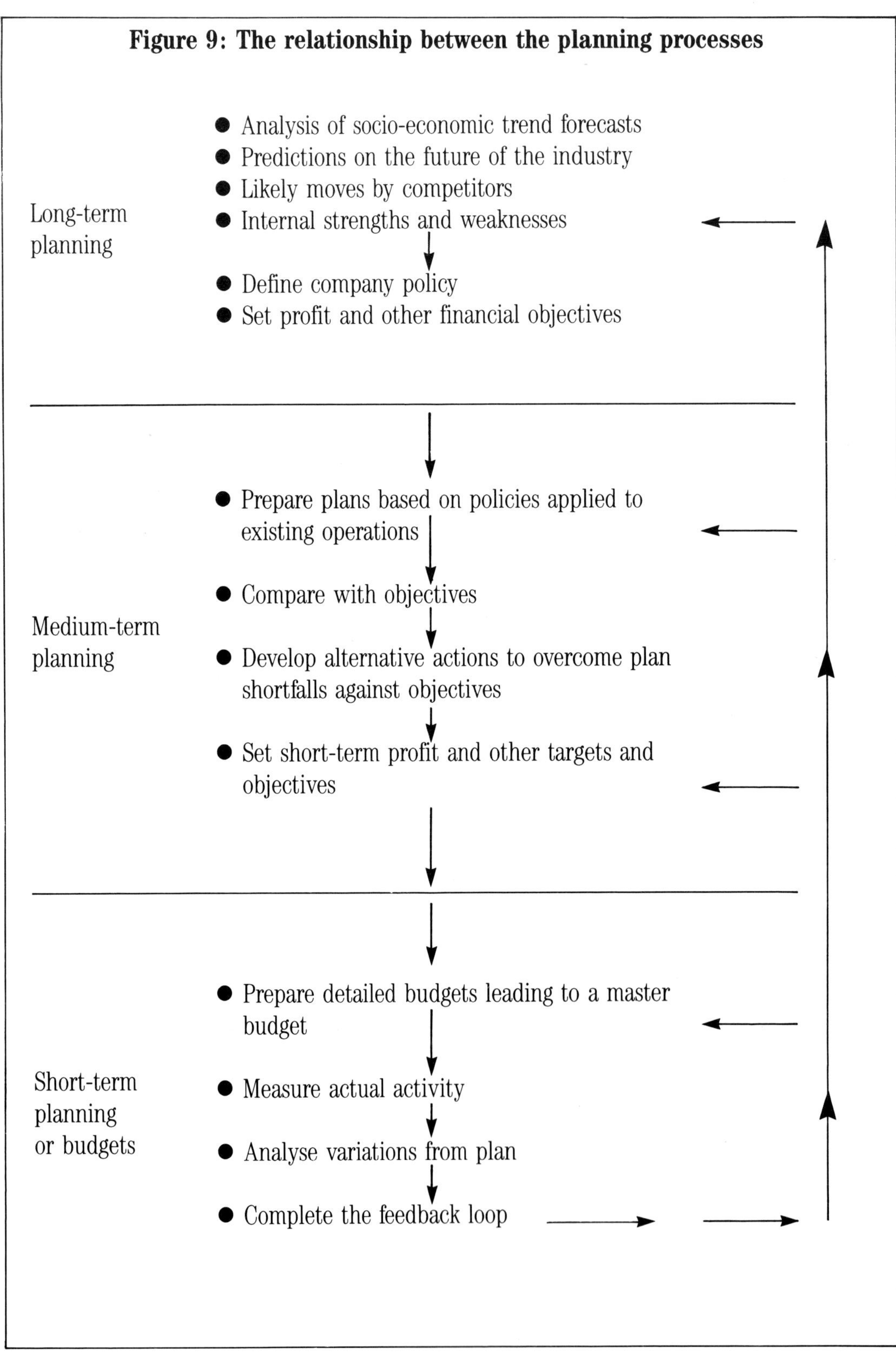

14.4 The budgeting process

In some companies, the budget is merely an annual document produced by the accountants without reference to the operational managers who will have to implement it. Because, in such cases, managers are not involved in the preparation of the budget, they are unlikely to be committed to fulfilling it. This results in copies of the budget lying ignored on managers' shelves gathering dust, with the budget playing no real part in business management.

Alternatively, the budget can represent a blueprint for management action and the future development of the business. As such, it is constantly referred to by managers and becomes central to business growth.

So what are the qualities necessary that make the budget part of the management process? What is your view? Write your answer below:

____

____

____

____

Now compare the views contained in your answer with the points raised in the text below.

The budgeting process must demonstrate a number of features in order for it to achieve its full use. First of all, it must be relevant to each manager concerned. To do this, it must be available at departmental, product, or process level. It must also portray the planned activity accurately. In some cases, budgets need to be flexible in order to take account of changed circumstances during the budget period.

Commitment to the process can be best obtained by making each manager responsible for preparing his own budgets. The budgets prepared should be based on company objectives and set realistic targets. They must be subject to senior management approval. Senior managers can then use the budget as a control document to monitor progress against the agreed actions.

In most cases, the budget process comprises a series of small budgets produced by department or process as appropriate. These small budgets are then consolidated to produce the overall company budget or *master budget*.

The budgeting process involves a series of consecutive events — the process cannot commence until the policy for future development is agreed — so the process itself needs to be planned. A flow chart of the major elements in a typical budgeting process is shown in the diagram overleaf.

Figure 10: Flow chart of a typical budgeting process

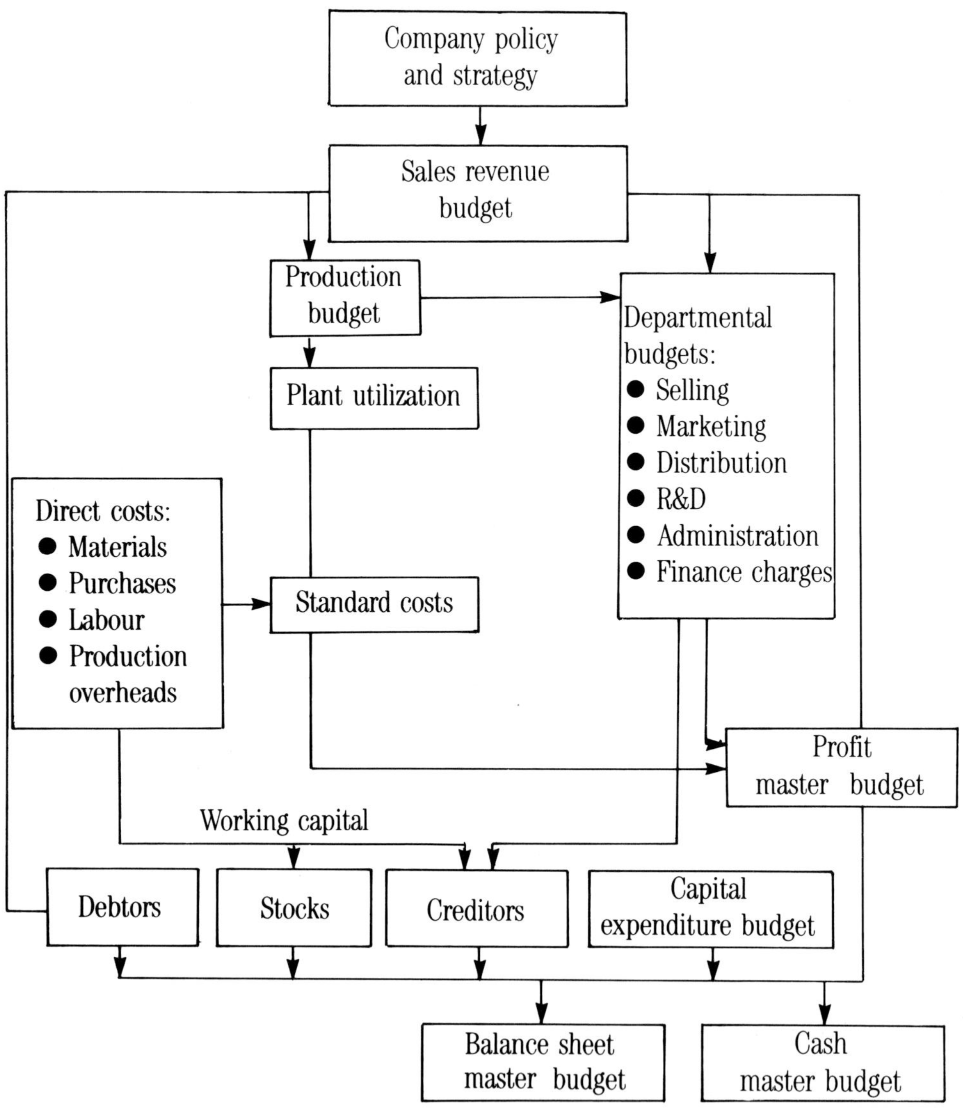

Company policy and strategy

Sales revenue budget

Production budget

Plant utilization

Departmental budgets:
- Selling
- Marketing
- Distribution
- R&D
- Administration
- Finance charges

Direct costs:
- Materials
- Purchases
- Labour
- Production overheads

Standard costs

Profit master budget

Working capital

Debtors

Stocks

Creditors

Capital expenditure budget

Balance sheet master budget

Cash master budget

The development of computerized planning and budgeting systems has been of great assistance in coping with the complexity of such processes. The scope of computerization ranges from the use of micro-computer based spreadsheet software in evaluating plan options to using large mainframes in handling the large databases produced.

In the following chapters the individual elements of this flow chart are discussed in more depth.

14.5 Limiting factors

The budget process is iterative, that is, some parts, called *limiting factors*, are repeated until a practical and reasonable overall budget is achieved and can be agreed.

These *limiting factors* can arise because of either internal or external conditions.

Consider the following internal limiting factors which might cause a sales forecast to be revised:

- Changes in production line capacity
- Inability to meet product quality or price standards
- Insufficient cash to fund expansion.

Similarly external factors affecting a sales forecast could be:

- Launch of a new competitive product
- Availability of suitable raw material
- Availability of qualified or skilled manpower.

Because of these kinds of limitation, the budget preparation process cannot be completed until the master budgets (profit and loss, balance sheet and cash) have been agreed.

Complete the exercise which follows before moving on.

Consider the area in which you currently work or another area which is familiar to you. Which are the three major factors that you believe limit improvement in efficiency and/or profit? Some suggestions are given below, but you may think of others.

(1) ______________________________

(2) ______________________________

(3) ______________________________

General limiting factors:

- Insufficient investment in plant and machinery
- Outdated work practices
- Lack of management direction
- Insufficient contribution from research and development (new and improved products)
- Poor sales and marketing
- Lack of good trained staff
- Inadequate attention to product quality
- Work flow problems such as bottlenecks limiting production
- Inflexible trade unions
- Insufficient attention to changes in the market place
- Inability to design product to a price.

There is obviously no 'right' answer to this question, it depends upon your own environment. However, it does indicate a way of thinking positively about improving a department or business, by removing obstacles to progress.

CHAPTER **15**

The key budgets

This chapter reviews the key departmental budgets that form part of a total business budgeting process.

15.1 The sales or revenue budget

The *sales* or *revenue budget* is the central budget as it determines both the expected company income and sale volumes that are to be achieved. In addition, many other departmental budgets relate directly to the sales volume — the exceptions being those with fixed costs only. Because of this, the sales budget has to be one of the first budgets agreed. The central position of the sales budget can be seen in the budget process flow chart which is repeated here.

Figure 11: Flow chart of a typical budgeting process

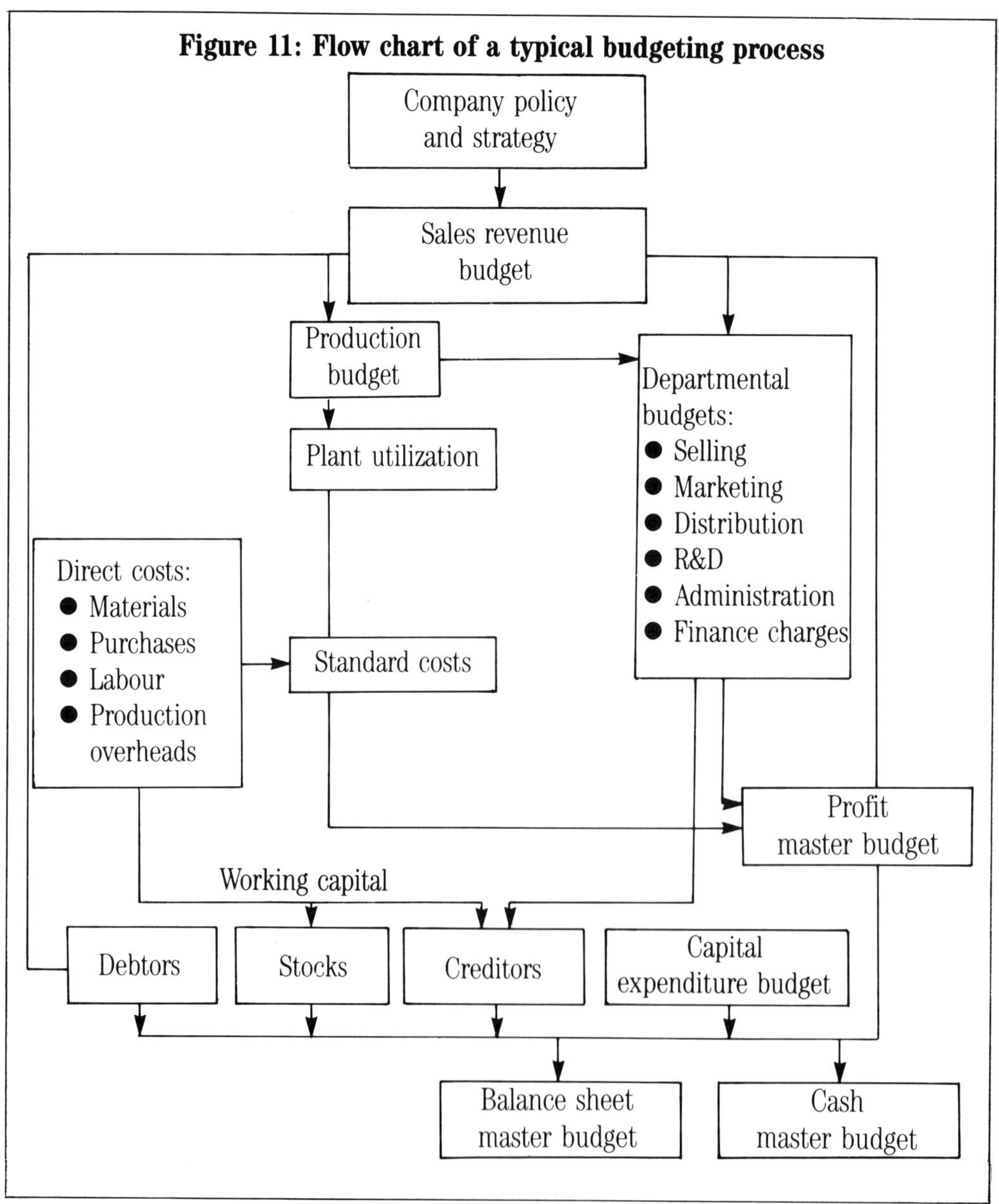

Sales and revenue are the most difficult areas to prepare accurate budgets and forecasts for. The main reason for this is that this is an area of business that is dependent on many factors outside the company's direct control.

Factors contributing to the sales budget

In preparing their budget, the sales and marketing staff must work together and consolidate their knowledge of the following areas:

- Market and industry trends:
  - ★ Consumers/customers
  - ★ Products
  - ★ Prices
- Likely moves and actions made by competitors
- Internal constraints (as reviewed)
- Company strategy:
  - ★ New products
  - ★ Distribution strategy
  - ★ Sales resources
  - ★ Advertising and promotion
  - ★ Pricing.

Because the forecast sales volume depends on the prices set, the size of the sales force, the amount of advertising, etc., these must be all be carefully matched. For example, an easy way of improving profit might appear to be a cut in the budgeted advertising expenditure. However, if the achievement of sales volume is closely related to advertising expenditure, an unbalanced and unachievable budget could result. It is important, also, to distinguish between sales *targets*, which are designed to motivate and encourage high levels of individual performance, and the sales *budget*, which is a reflection of likely achievement.

The sales forecast will normally be assembled on a monthly basis, so that volume requirements by month can be assessed. In this way, the seasonal peaks and troughs can be incorporated and dealt with. In the car industry, for example, companies need to reflect volume requirements for peak months such as those leading up to August when the new registration number appears.

Example

In this section a fictional manufacturing company, Great Engineering Ltd, is introduced in order to illustrate the way in which a sales budget is prepared. The same company will be used as a basis for developing other departmental budgets in the following sections.

You need to know that Great Engineering Ltd produces and sells three products — A, B and C. So, first of all, we must produce the sales budget based on anticipated sales as forecast by the sales manager:

Sales budget

Product	Sales forecast (units)	Average price achieved £	Revenue £'000
A	110,000	6.00	660.0
B	25,000	5.00	125.0
C	90,000	5.00	450.0
Sub-total			1235.0
Less: 2 per cent for product returns (faulty, etc.)			25.0
Sales revenue total:			1210.0

This sales budget will be reviewed in order, make the following checks:

- Whether the total revenue forecast is consistent with company growth objectives (Chapter 19). For example, the company may plan to increase sales by 10 per cent sales each year
- If the projected volumes are capable of being produced by the factory
- Whether the marketing department can support the volumes with advertising and promotional expenditure.

Once the sales budget has been given initial approval, the other departmental budgets can be completed as shown on the following pages. We will now move on to the production budget.

15.2 The production budget

If we now return to the budgeting process flow chart and move on from sales, we arrive at another core part of the overall budget — the production budget. Its key role in the budgeting process is self-evident from the flow chart. Non-manufacturing businesses normally have some kind of operating area which replaces production as the core activity in their own budgeting scheme.

The production budget (or its equivalent) is usually the most extensive budget produced because of the sheer number of activities that have to be represented. However, there are a number of factors that reduce the size of the task such as the presence of a standard costing system.

The production budget will most often be based on standard product specifications and costs. These standards are updated periodically and should contain current information and it should not be necessary to recost every factor from scratch. However, some factors will have to be adjusted for known changes such as inflation, pending pay awards and so on.

A production budget can usually be broken down into the following areas:

- Plant utilization
- Direct manpower costs
- Direct materials' costs.

Each of these is described below.

15.3 Plant utilization

It is likely that, in most manufacturing environments, each product will have been evaluated in work study terms. In other words, a product specification will have been drawn up, containing the average processing times for each operation.

Plant capacity can easily provide one of the major limitations to company expansion. We will now see how our sample company capacity matches against the sales projection.

Great Engineering's production department consists of three basic operations: pressing, turning and finishing. The work study department has provided us with the standard times for each operation (taking into account tooling up, maintenance and other down time) as follows:

Standard time for each operation (in minutes) per product

Product	*Process*		
	Pressing	*Turning*	*Finishing*
A	10	15	5
B	8	12	6
C	11	14	6

The plant utilization budget prepared is shown in the table below (based on the sales forecast developed previously).

Plant utilization budget

Product	*Sales volume*	*Machine hours*		
		Pressing	*Turning*	*Finishing*
	Units	*hours*	*hours*	*hours*
A	110,000	18,333	27,500	9,167
B	25,000	3,333	5,000	2,500
C	90,000	16,500	21,000	9,000
Total hours		38,166	53,500	20,667
Available hours		39,000	65,000	18,000
Capacity (excess)/surplus		834	11,500	(2,667)

From this we can conclude:

- Pressing is near to capacity and should be closely managed to prevent capacity problems
- There is adequate capacity in turning
- Capacity in finishing is inadequate to meet demand. This could be dealt with through:
  - ★ provision of extra machinery and staff
  - ★ additional overtime or extra shifts
  - ★ sub-contract
  - ★ downward revision of the sales budget.

In this case, the agreed solution is the provision of some additional equipment (through the capital budget) and additional overtime.

15.4 The direct labour budget

The budget for direct labour is derived by calculating the manpower required and then evaluating its cost. In practice, it is normally based on a system using standard times for each operation (as used in the last example). The total hours required are matched with available staff hours. The manpower requirement is then costed using the standard hourly cost of employment.

The available hours have to take account of all the factors which reduce total possible hours to available hours. These factors include holidays, average sickness, training and so on. Similarly, the standard costs per hour reflect full costs of employment including standard overtime, bonuses, National Insurance contributions, pension costs, etc. They may also include the cost of direct supervision.

Returning to Great Engineering, the direct labour cost budget can be calculated as shown below.

Direct labour budget

Department	*Machine hours*	*Equivalent man hours*	*Rate per hour*	*Total cost*	*No. of men*
			£	£	*(1,500 hrs p.a/man*
Pressing	38,166	38,166	2.50	95,415	26
Turning	53,500	17,833*	2.50	44,583	12
Finishing	18,000	18,000	2.00	36,000	12
Overtime	2,667	2,667	3.00	8,000	nil
	112,333	76,666		183,998	50

*Each man operates three machines in the turning area.

Note
The rate per hour is rate per productive hour. The cost of idle time and other non-productive time has been accounted for.

It is also possible to calculate the labour budget by product from the machine hours by process/by product table.

15.5 The direct materials budget

The budget for materials and components is derived from the sales budget after allowing for any stock movements that need to be taken into consideration.

Again, using a standard specification it is an easy job to multiply the unit requirements by the production volumes to give material and component volumes. The buyer must then check for any limitations and conditions that exist such as those following:

- That the materials and components are available when we want them and in the quantities and at the quality required
- The standard prices are realistic
- The availability of alternative supplies.

If all conditions are satisfactory we can cost out the volume requirements using standard prices.

Great Engineering's direct materials budget calculation is shown below.

Direct materials budget
Volume and cost
Volume requirement

Material/ Component	*Product* A	*B*	*C*	*Total usage*	*Scrap*	*Total needed*
Blanks for pressing	110,000	25,000	90,000	225,000	11,250	236,250
Component 1	220,000	nil	180,000	400,000	8,000	408,000
Component 2	110,000	25,000	nil	135,000	2,700	137,700
Component 3	nil	50,000	90,000	140,000	2,800	142,800

Cost of materials/components

Material/ component	*Total needed*	*Item cost*	*Total cost*
		£	£
Blanks	236,250	1.35	318,937
Component 1	408,000	0.40	16,320
Component 2	137,700	0.05	6,885
Component 3	142,800	0.045	6,426
			348,568

Note
Scrap rate: 5 per cent on blanks and 2 per cent on components.

15.6 Buffer budgets

In preparing our budgets so far, we have assumed that the company works on a continuous basis. In other words, that there are no timing differences between buying, manufacture and sales. However, in reality, we use stocks of raw materials, work in progress and finished goods to smooth the flow of business. To take raw materials and components as an example, the cost of stopping flow-line production because of a shortage of materials can be very high. On the other hand, it is also expensive to hold large stocks of raw materials. Part of the planning process has to involve establishing agreed stock levels. This involves balancing the cost of holding stock, the time taken from order to delivery, and the consequences of running out of raw materials. Similarly, we need to establish sensible *buffer stocks* between different production processes. In this way we can smooth production flows.

Finally, we need to carry sufficient finished goods stocks to meet immediate customer demand although the requirement for this depends on the product manufactured. Obviously, we would not hold finished goods stocks of specialized high-priced manufactured products.

The location of buffer stocks is illustrated in the diagram below:

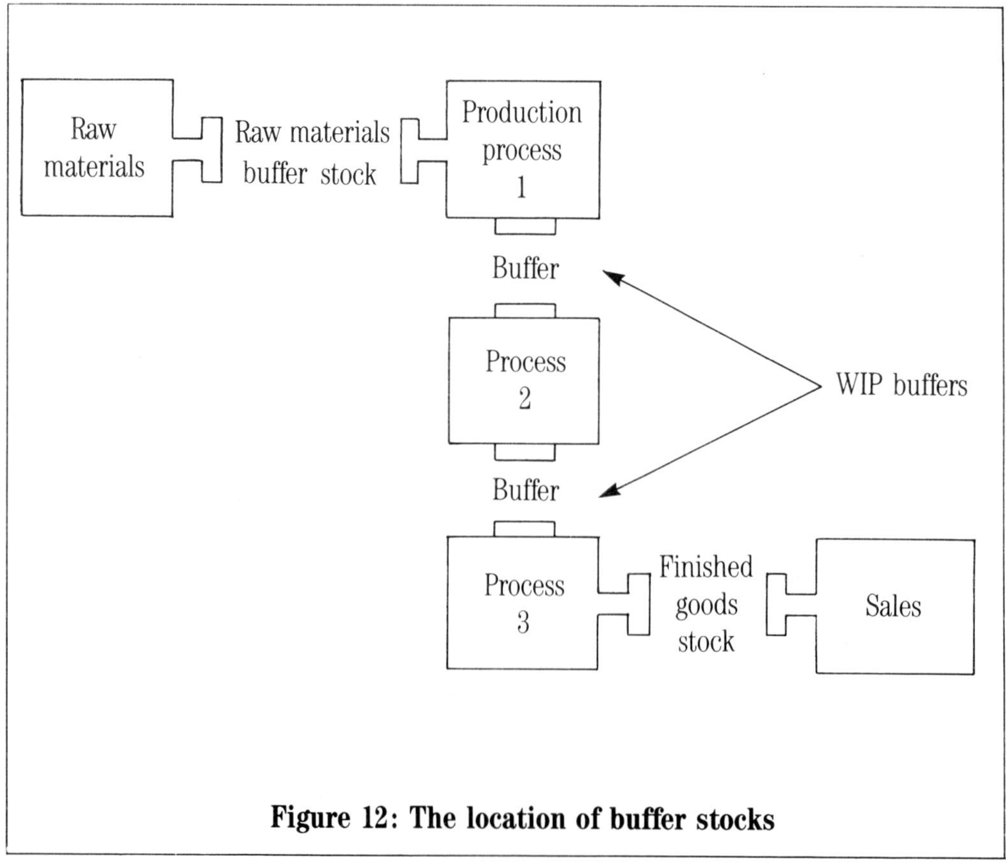

Figure 12: The location of buffer stocks

15.7 Overhead and departmental budgets

At the same time as the main production budgets are being assembled, the overhead and departmental budgets can be started. A budget should be prepared for each major cost centre. The budget formats illustrated here are typical of those in common use. As you will see, the areas shown usually come under the control of a single director or senior manager.

The following pages show sample formats indicating the main cost headings commonly found in each area. Once again in a practical situation, the headings used reflect actual costs incurred.

The formats shown are:

- The *Production overheads budget* (*fig. a*)
- The *Sales and marketing department budget* (*fig. b*)
- The *Distribution budget* (*fig. c*)
- The *Research and development budget* (*fig. d*)
- *Budgets for other administrative and central departments* (*fig. e*)

Self-assessment exercise
If you have access to your own department's budget, compare its structure and content with the examples provided here.

Alternatively, assume that you are starting a budget from scratch for your own department or one which is familiar to you. Write down the major cost headings that would be needed on the format given below.

Major cost headings for the ______________________ department

Manpower

____

____

____

____

Materials or supplies

____

____

____

____

____

Other goods and services

____

____

____

Now compare your answers to the examples on the following pages.

Figure a: Production overhead budget format

	Last year's budget £	*Last year's actual* £	*Proposed budget* £
Materials			
Cleaning materials			
Oils and lubricants			
Tools			
Other			
Labour			
Management and supervisory			
Maintenance			
Work study			
Cleaners			
Services			
Computer services charge			
Power, light, heat and water			
Premises and plant			
Rent and rates			
Insurance			
Depreciation			
Others			
Head office charges			
Total			

Figure b: Sales and marketing department budget format

	Last year's budget £	*Last year's actual* £	*Proposed budget* £
Sales labour			
Salaries			
Commission			
Cars			
Travel and entertainment			
Sales office			
Office supplies			
Wages and salaries			
Postage			
Telephone			
Premises costs			
Marketing			
Salaries			
Office costs			
Sales brochures			
Exhibition costs			
Advertising			
Press			
TV			
Radio			
Direct mail			
Public relations			
Total			

Figure c: Distribution budget format

	Last year's budget £	*Last year's actual* £	*Proposed budget* £
Warehouse			
Packing materials			
Salaries and wages			
Equipment costs			
Forklift truck costs			
Premises costs			
Transport			
Salaries and wages			
Vehicle costs			
Fuel			
Maintenance			
Tax and insurance			
Contract hire			
Depot costs			
Total			

Figure d: Research and development department budget

	Projects						*Total*
	A1	*A2*	*B1*	*C1*	*C2*	*C3*	
Project costs							
Materials							
Raw materials							
Tools							
Other							
Labour							
Engineers							
Technicians							
Others							
Expenses							
Consultancy fees							
Sub totals							
General costs							
Supervisory salaries							
Laboratory costs							
Plant depreciation							
Premises costs							
Other costs							
Total							

Budget format for other administrative and central departments

Each administrative and central department will have similar budget formats, with one or two lines relevant to the particular department. For example, the personnel department will include specific lines for advertising and recruitment expenditure.

The departmental budgets falling into this category can use a generalized format as in the example below. Typical departments using such a format include:

- General Manager's office
- Finance and Administration departments
- Company secretary's office
- Personnel and Training
- Management services
- Work study
- Quality department
- Buying department, etc.

Figure e: Format for other administrative and central departments

	Last year's budget £	*Last year's actual* £	*Proposed budget* £
Departmental costs			
Materials			
Contracts			
Other			
Labour			
Management and supervisory			
Clerical			
Others			
Other expenses			
Premises costs			
Office equipment			
hire			
depreciation			
supplies			
Telephone			
Postage			
Travel and entertainment			
Other expenses			
Allocations			
Management services			
Premises department etc.			
Total			
Recharges to other depts			
Net total budget			

15.8 The capital expenditure budget

Before moving on to the consolidation of the profit and loss budgets, we also need to consider a budget that is assembled alongside the departmental budgets — the *capital expenditure* budget. Again, this budget needs detailed input from departmental managers.

The capital expenditure budget is an expression of forecast cash expenditure on fixed assets. This is used in order to estimate movements in balance sheet fixed assets and hence allow projections for the profit and loss depreciation charge to be made.

The budget is prepared by assembling information from two major sources:

- The list of approved capital projects for which expenditure is still outstanding. The remaining expenditure can be projected over the budget period.

  For example, if a new factory costing £1.2 million had been approved, and construction had commenced in 198X, the cash flows might be £0.4m in 198X, £0.5m in 198Y and £0.3m in 198Z. The 198Y budget would show the £0.5m payments forecast for that year.
- The estimated expenditure on new approvals likely to be made during the year. As well as new building and plant projects, this would include items such as replacement vehicles, office equipment etc., which are purchased on a much shorter time scale.

A sample capital expenditure budget format appears below.

Capital expenditure budget

	Expenditure projection					
	Jan	*Feb*	*Mar*	*Apr . . .*	*Dec*	*Total*
Projects approved but not completed						
Buildings						
Project register No. 1						
Payments						
Plant						
Approval register No. 23						
Payments						
Approval register No. 15						
Payments						
Items forecast but not approved to date						
New delivery vans						
Payments						
Office equipment						
Payments						
New automatic press						
Payments						
Total						

CHAPTER **16**

The master budgets

This chapter shows how the master budgets are prepared to complete the budgeting process.

The final exercise at the end of the budgeting process is the preparation of the master budgets. These master budgets are prepared by consolidating the information contained in the individual budgets. They also represent an assessment of the overall financial outcomes if the plan is achieved.

The master budgets therefore comprise:

- The profit and loss budget
- The budget balance sheet
- The cash budget.

These can only be prepared once the sales, production and departmental budgets are fully completed.

16.1 Master budget 1 — the profit and loss account

The profit and loss budget is constructed in the standard style we have already seen used for reporting accounts. The easiest way of demonstrating this is to use an example. Again, we will illustrate the budget by using figures from our example company Great Engineering Ltd. In addition to the sales and production (materials and labour) figures already produced, we have the following overhead budget information for the year:

	£'000
Production overhead	210
Sales and marketing	92
Administration and central costs	103
Research and development	51
Finance charges (taxation, interest dividends, etc.)	85

Note

These overhead and departmental costs include the costs of provisions for depreciation and for items such as bad debts and stock write-offs.

The completed budget is shown opposite.

Profit and loss master budget:
Great Engineering Ltd.

	£'000	£'000
Sales		1210
Direct costs		
Labour	184	
Materials	347	
Production overhead	210	
		741
		469
Selling and overhead expenditure		
Sales and marketing	92	
Distribution	65	
Administration and central costs	103	
R&D	51	
		311
Budgeted trading profit		158
Finance and other charges		85
Budgeted retained earnings		73

Often, at the first attempt, the budget trading profit is unsatisfactory, which normally means too low. If this occurs, management will have to look at the possibilities of implementing alternative strategies. This involves recosting the budgets.

In some companies, several 'activity cases' utilizing different strategies may be costed in order to achieve the optimum results in the next financial period. The use of computerized planning and budgeting models makes this type of approach much easier.

16.2 Master budget 2 — the balance sheet

Following approval of the profit and loss budget the closing balance sheet can be projected.

The balance sheet budget is completed by following the sequence shown in the diagram overleaf. The opening balance sheet (which is the previous year's closing balance sheet) is the base point.

Balance sheet projection method

Opening balance	*Movement in funds*	*Closing balance*
(1) *Fixed assets*		
Cost	*Add*: Capital expenditure *Deduct*: Cost of disposals	Fixed asset costs
Accumulated depreciation	*Add*: P&L depreciation charge *Deduct*: Accumulated depreciation on disposals	Accumulated depreciation
(2) *Working capital*		
Stocks and WIP	Set realistic closing figures consistent with process costs and sales	Closing stocks and WIP
Debtors	*Add*: Invoicing *Deduct*: Cash receipts estimates and write-offs	Debtors
Creditors	*Add*: P&L Expenditure, wages, purchases, expenses etc. *Deduct*: Payment	Creditors
Taxation and dividend creditors	*Add*: P&L charge *Deduct*: Payment	Taxation and dividend owing
Cash	Await the outcome of the cash budget	Cash
(3) *Equity and loan capital*		
	Any known movement — issues, borrowings or repayments	First estimate pending cash budget

Following this exercise, the balance sheet can be assembled. Note that the values calculated as balance sheet movements also form the basis for the cash master budget.

16.3 Master budget 3 — the cash budget

The cash budget is completed using standard cash flow statements. The format is as follows.

The cash flow budget

	£	£
Profit before taxation (from P&L budget)		
Add: Depreciation		
Proceeds from sale of fixed assets		
Proceeds from new capital	___	
		___
Funds generated		===
Applications		
Capital expenditure (from capital budget)		
Investments purchased		
Payment of taxation and dividends		
Repayment of capital/loans		
Increases/(decreases) in current assets		
(Increase)/decrease in liabilities		
Stocks and WIP		
Debtors		
Creditors	___	
		___
Cash surplus or (deficit)		===

This budget is necessary in order to discover the future cash and funding requirements needed by the business. If a cash deficit is predicted which is outside the company's borrowing limits, action must be taken. Either the limits must be renegotiated or the plan reworked to produce better cash utilization.

The advantage of a plan such as this, particularly if the cash plan is produced on a month by month basis, is that management can anticipate cash highs and lows and take appropriate action.

Now test your own ability to produce a cash budget by completing Exercise 15.

Exercise 15

Using Great Engineering's budget results given below, produce a cash flow forecast for the next period, using the format provided.

In addition to the retained earnings figure of £73K shown on the P&L master budget, you are given the following extra information to complete the cash budget:

- The taxation and dividends charge for the year totals £70K. (Profit before tax therefore equals £73K + £70K = £143K.)
- Taxation and dividends to be paid equal £64K. (Note these are the previous year's charges being paid.)
- Capital expenditure is forecast at £85K
- The depreciation charge for the year is £34K
- £10K will be received from the sale of fixed assets
- A bank loan of £25K is due to be repaid
- There is no change to equity or loan capital or stocks and WIP. No investments are envisaged
- Debtors will increase by £15K and creditors by £10K.

Cash budget for Great Engineering Ltd

	£K	£K
Profit before tax (from P&L budget)		[ ]
Add: Depreciation	[ ]	
Proceeds from sale of fixed assets	[ ]	
Proceeds from new capital	nil	
		[ ]
Funds generated		187
Applications		
Capital expenditure (from capital budget)		[ ]
Investments purchased		nil
Taxation and dividend payments		[ ]
Repayment of capital/loans		[ ]
Increases/(decreases) in current assets (Increase)/decrease in liabilities:		
Stocks and WIP	nil	
Debtors	[ ]	
Creditors	( )	
		5
Cash surplus or (deficit)		8

CHAPTER 17

Managing the budgeting process

This chapter deals with the methods that are used to keep the budgeting process effective and realistic.

Budgets are only of value if they really do reflect company intention for future development and have the proper staff commitment. Otherwise they are merely time-consuming and wasteful paper exercises.

Consider the following complaints:

'The budget costs are just a 10 per cent increase on the previous year's figures.'

'The sales figures are "wishful thinking".'

'The departmental costs are padded to enable managers to "perform" by beating their budgets.'

In each case, it is unlikely that the budgeting process will form an action plan for company development.

17.1 The construction of realistic budgets

In terms of performance standards, the budget should reflect average likely performance — results achievable in normal circumstances. It should not reflect 'stretch targets' set for maximum possible performance which there is only a small chance of achieving. Neither should the budget be allowed to support and maintain outdated and outmoded practices. In other words, if it is a conservative document, which merely represents an extension of previous performance, it is unlikely that new ideas will be incorporated and progress made.

In constructing a budget we have to create a balance between building the whole budget up from scratch — *zero-based budgeting* — and carrying forward past standards.

It is obviously expedient to carry forward standards, and, in this respect, the unit cost standards and work study standards can form a useful base for budget development. This must be on the understanding that the standards are continually updated to reflect improvements and efficiencies as they are identified.

Zero-based budgeting is a valuable technique if it is used selectively. As the name suggests, it involves starting your budget from a zero-base each time rather than basing it on last year's figures. Each cost has then to be justified in its own right. It is a technique that can be used when it appears that inefficiencies, slackness or even deliberate 'padding' are present in the budgeted figures.

Another useful factor in budget preparation is the presence of some kind of *management by objectives* system within the company. If each manager has a clear idea of his departmental objectives it provides a clearer framework for budget preparation. An alternative way of reviewing departmental budget results is through a 'benchmarking' process. By this process, results are compared with equivalent costs in other companies known for their efficient and effective practices. Some common factor for such comparisons, such as cost as a percentage of revenue, has to be used in order for the comparison to be made. The Centre for Interfirm Comparisons can provide ready-made data of this nature.

17.2 Sensitivity analysis

If the budget is to be a blueprint for future company development, management ought to have some idea of the validity of the assumptions underlying the budget. It has been said that the only certainty in a forecast is that it will be wrong to some extent!

Sensitivity analysis involves reviewing the key assumptions underlying the budget, and checking their validity. This can be performed in several different ways. For example, we can use statistical analysis to determine the possibility of future events happening.

As another example, we might consider one of the key elements of the profit budget — the sales revenue forecast. We can then consider the implications of the following:

- a sales volume shortfall by 10 per cent
- a sales volume excess by 10 per cent
- the late introduction of the next price increase.

Analysis of these types of factors should expose potential weaknesses in the budget. As a consequence, *contingency plans* can be drawn up to either minimize the effects of such events, or provide alternative strategies and actions. In most circumstances, it is only possible to analyse the key assumptions in this way because of time constraints. Nevertheless, such analysis forms an important validating role in the budgeting process.

PART 4

The use of finance in management

CHAPTER 18

Measuring performance against budget - variance analysis

This chapter describes the use of variance analysis as a control mechanism for management.

In the last four chapters we have covered the preparation and completion of plans and budgets. But, the management process does not stop with the completion of the final master budgets, which only represent the desired financial results.

In order to achieve the financial results the underlying plans and actions assumed in the preparation of the budgets must be implemented. In this unit we investigate how actual performance results are used in monitoring performance against an agreed budget. In particular we will be concentrating on a technique called *variance analysis*.

18.1 What is variance analysis?

The first step in understanding variance analysis is to understand what a variance is. The standard definition of a variance is:

A variance represents the difference between actual and planned performance.

For example:

- If the sales budget for July was 10,000 units and we sold 9,500 units, a variance of 500 units would have occurred.
- If, in the same month, we had planned to spend £100,000 on advertising and we actually spent £80,000, a variance of £20,000 would have been produced.

Variances occur in two forms:

- *Unfavourable, adverse* or *negative variances* — when revenue is lower, or cost higher, than planned leading to a worse profit result (as in the first example above).
- *Favourable,* or *positive variances* — when revenue is higher, or cost lower, than anticipated or planned leading to a better profit result (as in the second example above).

By analysing variances, we can understand the reasons why *actual* performance differs from *planned* performance.

In the case of *favourable* variances, we want to understand the causes of variances in order to sustain or recreate the same favourable business conditions in the future. For example, we might find that a favourable sales revenue variance is being caused by higher prices being charged than originally planned. It is possible that we underestimated market prices and can continue to sustain high prices without reducing sales volume.

Conversely, by locating the causes of unfavourable conditions, we can attempt to minimize or avoid such effects in the future. For instance, a situation might occur in which an adverse sales volume variance is found to be caused poor product quality. Action can then be taken to remedy the situation.

Variance analysis can be a difficult concept to understand unless approached logically, because, in a given practical situation, many variables exist.

In the sales variance example given above, the adverse variance could be caused by many different reasons. These could include overpricing, stock shortage, bad salesmanship, competitors' activity, and many others, in addition to the quality problem mentioned. As the causes of variances are many, it is important to approach the analysis systematically. Let us now look at an example of a management report, and investigate the approach to variance analysis.

18.2 Using variance analysis

The use of variance analysis can be best illustrated by an example. The table of results (below) is a typical example of a profit and loss summary statement used in a small engineering company (or in a subsidiary profit centre of a large company). The company board will expect such results, when formally presented, to be accompanied by a full explanation of variances from plan.

As you can see, the three columns shown represent the plan, the actual results and the variance (the difference between plan and actual). In the variance column, adverse variances are shown in brackets. If you look at the bottom line of the table you can also see that against, a budgeted profit of £320,000 for the quarter, the company has made £285,000. This represents a *profit shortfall*, or *adverse profit variance*, of £35,000.

In the remainder of this chapter, you will learn the way in which this overall variance can be analysed.

Profit and loss statement — (Quarter 1)

	Plan £'000	*Actual* £'000	*Variance* £'000
Sales	7,500	7,350	(150)
Cost of sales			
Ex-factory cost	6,550	6,450	100
Stock movement	50	50	nil
Factory costs	6,600	6,500	100
Selling costs	325	305	20
Administration and other	275	300	(25)
Total cost	7,200	7,105	95
Selling profit	300	245	(55)
Factory variance	20	40	20
Profit	320	285	(35)

Notes

- The adverse variances are shown in brackets
- In this example the profit statement is constructed using the following guidelines:
  - ★ Product is transferred into sales stock at an ex-factory standard cost per unit (actual units × standard cost)
  - ★ Selling profit is sales revenue less cost of sales of units sold (units sold × standard cost) and after selling and administration costs
  - ★ Factory variance is the difference between product transferred at standard cost, and production at actual cost
  - ★ Company profit is therefore selling profit, plus or minus factory variance.

From the table, you can begin to build up some ideas on the causes of the adverse variance. For example, it appears from simple inspection that the adverse variance on the sales line (\$150,000 adverse) warrants immediate investigation. Whereas the favourable factory variance (\$20,000 favourable) indicates that production is going well. The approach to variance analysis therefore commences with the profit variance being split into its constituent parts. This is illustrated, in diagrammatic form, as follows:

Figure 13: Variance chart

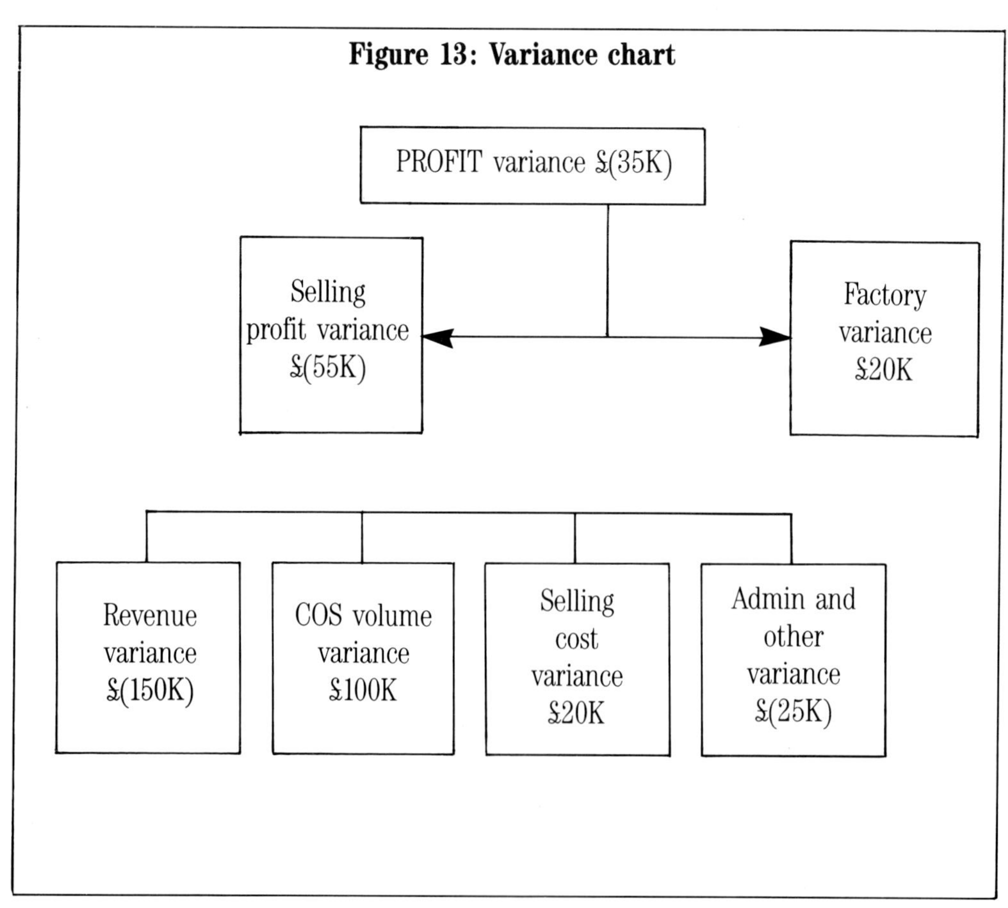

However this simple analysis only starts to tell us *where* the variance is — it does not tell *why* it is happening. To discover the 'whys', each of these major variances has to be split still further into its constituent parts. In the following pages, the major sales and production variances are discussed in more depth.

In practice, priority is always given to locating the cause of the largest or most significant variance first. So, in this case we will start by investigating the sales or revenue variance.

18.3 Sales variances

The sales variance is itself built up of three major types of variance. Each is listed below together with its method of calculation:

- *Price variance* — Sales prices vary from planned price

  (Actual price – Plan price) × Actual volume

- *Volume variance* — Sales volumes vary from planned levels

  (Actual volume – Plan volume) × Plan price

- *Mix variance* — This occurs in multi-product companies and reflects a different balance between sales of each product type to that planned.

To return to our example, a single product company, we find that further investigation of sales performance reveals the following data:

	Plan	*Actual*
Sales volume (units)	375,000	366,500
Average unit price	£20.00	£20.054

From this the sales variance of £150K can be analysed as follows (N.B. K = '000):

Volume variance = (375,000 – 366,500) × £20.00 =	(£170K)
Price variance = £(20.054 – 20.00) × 375,000 =	£20K (approx)
Total sales variance:	(£150K)

N.B. In a single product company there is no sales mix variance.

From this you can see that the adverse sales variance of £150,000 has been caused by an under-achievement in units sold producing an adverse variance of £170,000. This has been offset to a small degree by a favourable price variance (£20,000) resulting from a higher-than-plan average achieved price per unit.

The *reason* for the volume shortfall obviously needs to be pursued further. Additional information will be required in order to provide further analysis, for example to discover whether it results from poor sales force management or whatever.

An important factor to note at this stage is that items such as volume variances will affect all the variable costs throughout the organization. For example, the £170,000 adverse volume variance in sales revenue shown above, is offset to a certain extent, by a £100,000 favourable variance in cost of sales. It is also likely that other favourable cost variances are produced in the selling and administration costs — the payment of lower-than-plan commission to sales staff being a typical example.

Exercise 16

The annual sales plan of a car manufacturer, and the results achieved were as follows:

		Volume units	*Average dealer price £*	*Revenue £million*
1986 plan	Model A	10,000	4,500	45.0
1986 actual	Model A	9,500	5,000	47.5
Variances		(500)	500	2.5

You are asked to calculate the sales volume and price variances using the following format.

				£m
Price variance	= Unit price variance	×	Actual volume	
	= £ [ ]	×	9,500	= [ ]
Volume variance	= Volume difference	×	Planned price	
	= [( )]	×	£4,500	= [( )]
Total revenue variance (price less volume)				= £2.5m

Now check your answer with the solution in the back of the book.

18.4 Factory or production variances

The next area of major variances usually occurs in the factory or production function. This is because production normally represents the biggest single expenditure area in a company and therefore generates the most significant cost variances.

The initial variance analysis is based on the major cost areas. These are:

- Raw materials and components
- Labour costs
- Overheads

Figure 14: Production variance chart

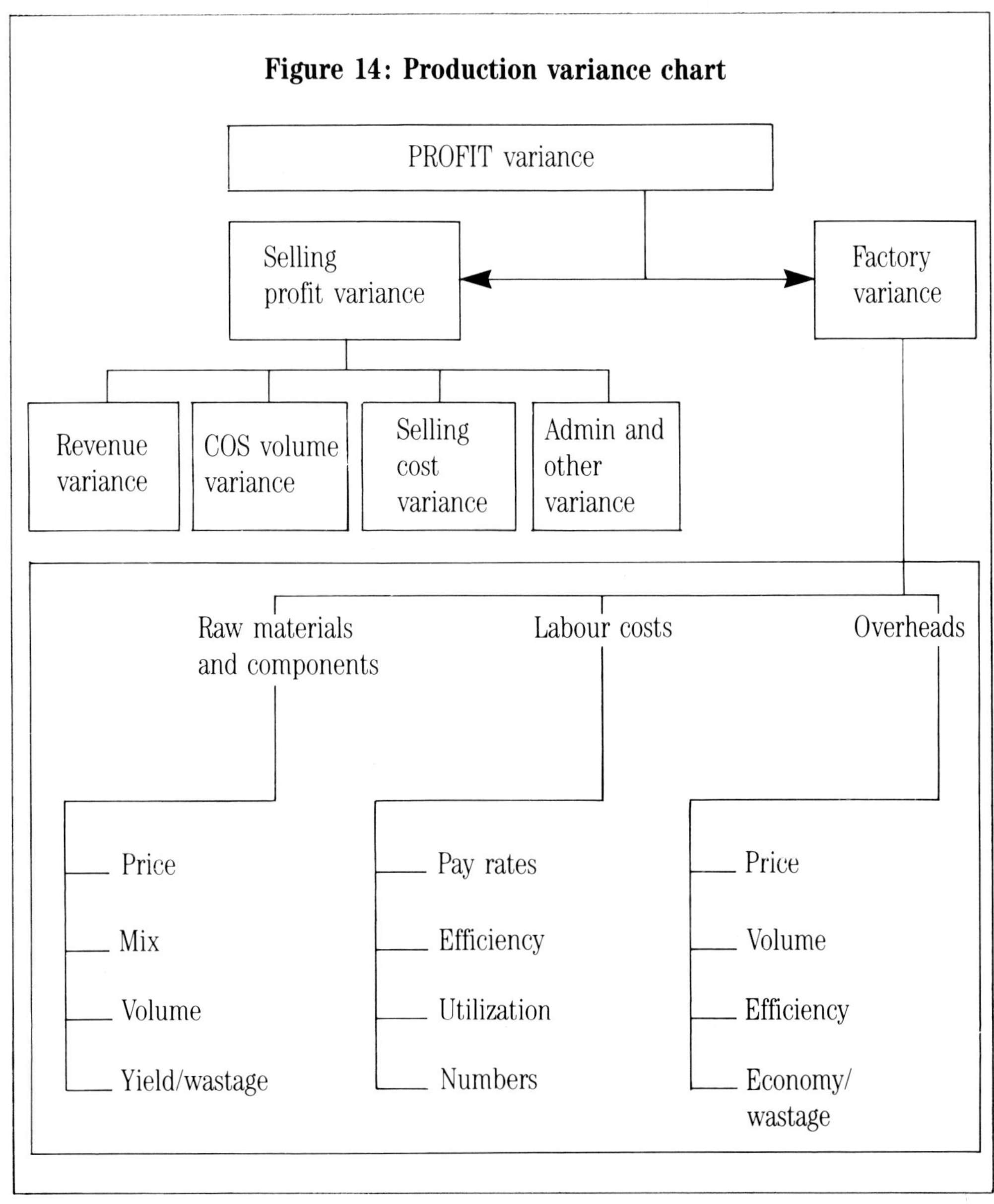

Each of these cost areas has a number of key elements which may be measured as *causal variances*. The table overleaf demonstrates the key elements which make up production variances, describes how they are caused, and indicates the person normally responsible for managing the activity.

Table of production variances

Variance	*Cause*	*Manager*
• *Material/components*		
(1) Price variance	Increase or decrease in actual price over standard	Buyer
(2) Usage variance	More or less material used than in the product standard.	Production
(3) Yield variance	More or less product produced per standard input.	Production
(4) Mix variance	Change in standard cost caused by differing mix of materials or components.	Production/ Engineering
(5) Scrap/wastage variance	Increase or decrease of scrap/wastage over standard.	Production/ Buyer
• *Direct labour*		
(1) Pay rate variance	A difference in pay rates compared with standard.	Various
(2) Idle-time/Utilization variance	The standard wages cost of non-standard idle time.	Production
(3) Efficiency variance	The difference between actual output per man and standard output.	Production
(4) Labour mix variance	The use of different grade manpower from the standard.	Production
(5) Available time variance	The standard wages cost of paid time lost through public holidays and similar events.	—
• *Variable overheads*		
(1) Price or cost variance	Increase or decrease compared with standard.	Buyer
(2) Usage variance	The usage of items such as electrical power compared with standard consumption.	Production

- *Fixed overheads*

(1) Price or cost variance	Increase or decrease over standard expenditure.	All
(2) Capacity variance	Change from planned capacity.	MD
(3) Labour variances	Causes as for direct labour above.	Department Managers

18.5 Variance analysis summary

Variance analysis may seem involved and complex, but when it is approached in a logical and systematic way, it is a fast and effective method of detecting the causes of both favourable and unfavourable trends in business. In addition, it is not necessary to perform detailed analysis of *each* variance all the time. Usually management will only require the significant and most costly variance trends to be analysed. This is known as *analysis by exception*.

In our review of variance analysis, we have only dealt in depth with sales and production department variances. This is because fluctuations in revenue and direct costs usually produce the most significant variances. Indeed, where revenue and variable costs are concerned, quite small variances in unit costs or unit prices can have very significant effects when accompanied by large production volumes.

Each overhead and indirect department producing budgets or plans should, however, be subject to review of its current performance against plan on a periodic basis. Because most will consist primarily of fixed costs, the causal analysis should be easier to determine.

Finally, the value of variance analysis is helped considerably by the production of good standards and plans. If these latter items are not good estimates, a great deal of variance analysis time will be spent detecting plan errors, and variances will be devalued as business trend control factors.

A summary of the way in which variances occur is shown in the figure that follows.

Note
The particular variances shown overleaf are not necessarily the key causes in any particular instance, but are the most commonly occurring types.

Figure 15: Full variance chart

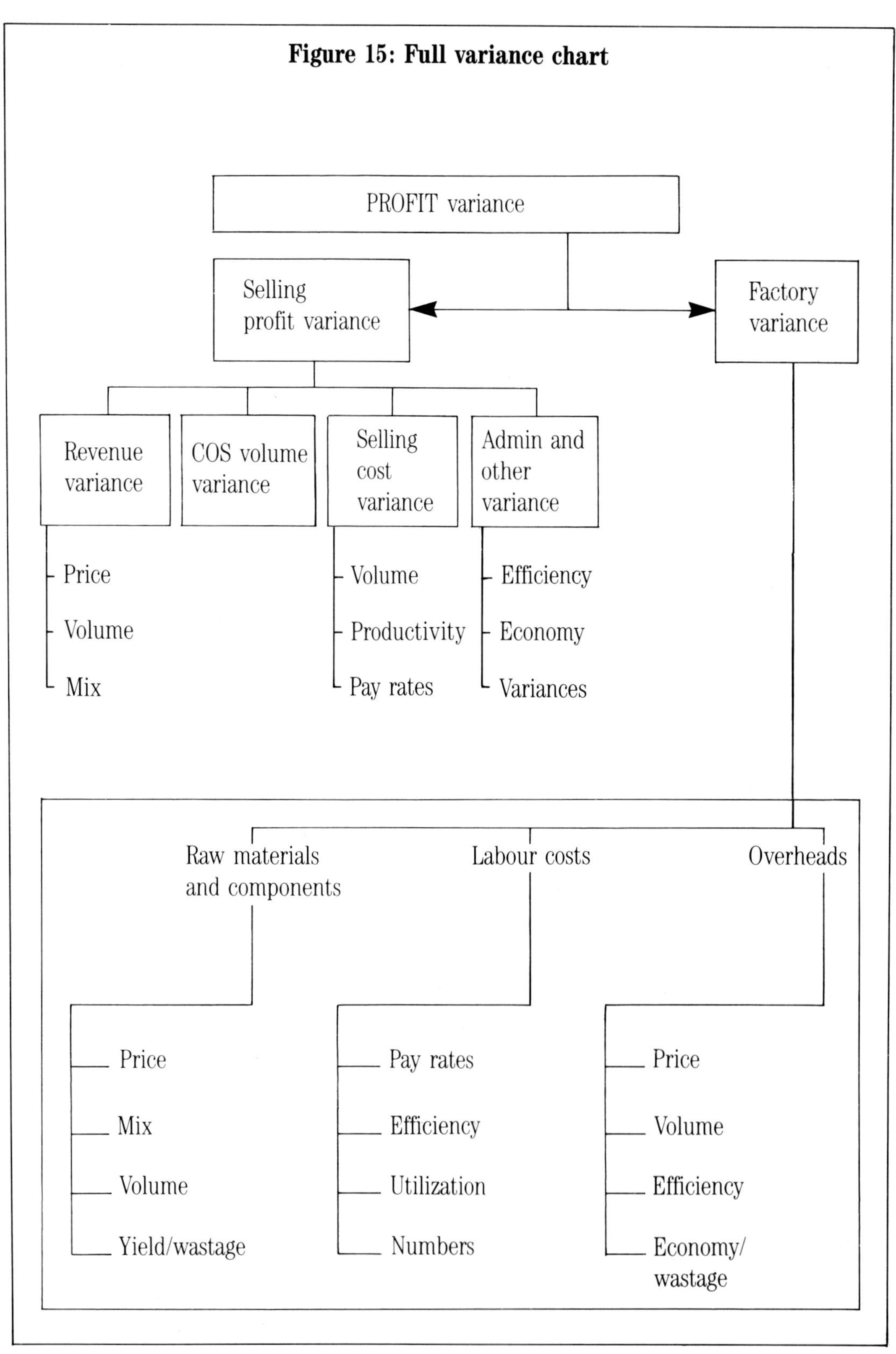

CHAPTER 19

The key management measures

This chapter presents the key measures used by management in measuring business performance. It also demonstrates how they are calculated.

An important aid to the successful management of a company is the identification of the key measures which indicate the state or condition of the company. This chapter summarizes the key measures commonly used by management *within* a company.

For comparison, we will consider some of the key measures we might use in measuring personal financial performance. Don't forget that we, as individuals, have to make decisions with our own income and assets, just as companies do. For example, with our own income, once we have covered our essential costs, we have to decide on how we would like to spend the remainder. In other words, we must strike a balance between how much we spend in various ways, such as:

- *Optional expenditure* — entertainment, new clothes
- *Maintaining our existing assets* — redecorating the house, servicing the car
- *Investing in the future* — savings, a pension plan.

Because of their value in representing the condition of a company, the key measures shown below are often used as prime company objectives and are therefore of fundamental significance.

19.1 Profit

Well, you wouldn't expect to get very far before it is mentioned! However, profit may be expressed in several different ways (various definitions were given in Chapter 8). However, unless otherwise defined, profit usually means profit *before* tax and interest.

Profit is obviously a key result in absolute terms. It is also widely used as a base for the indices shown below, in which it is known as *return*, as in *return* on capital employed. Whilst ideally, profit is the highest value possible, it should always be remembered that the profit and loss account contains some 'investment' items, such as research and development costs, plant and building maintenance, training costs and so on. These costs are essential for the long-term growth of the company.

Profit planning is always therefore a balancing act between short-term profit generation and long-term investment. Note how this compares with the decisions on personal income shown above.

19.2 Return on capital employed (ROCE) and return on assets (ROA)

When we invest our own money, we always want to know what we are going to get in return. For example, if we have to choose between investing money in a building society or a bank we will compare the interest rates paid to investors by each. *Return on capital employed* (*ROCE*) and

Return on assets (*ROA*) are similar yardsticks for a business. They measure the return or profit achieved on the investment *in* the company or *by* the company. The two terms are similar, as you will see in the definitions below:

- *Return* is the profit before tax and interest (common to both)
- *Capital employed* is the total investment in the company as shown by the balance sheet (usually averaged over the period). This of course is often equal to:
- *Assets* which are the net investment by the company — the opposite side of the balance sheet.

The basic equation for calculating this figure is therefore:

$$ROCE = \frac{\text{Profit}}{\text{Capital employed}}$$

or

$$ROA = \frac{\text{Profit}}{\text{Assets}}$$

The capital employed or assets are usually averaged by adding the opening and closing figures and then halving the result. The result of the equation is then usually expressed as a percentage, e.g. 10 per cent ROA, which, of course, is the same way that building society or bank interest is expressed.

The importance of this figure derives from the fact that it is a basic measure of the efficiency with which the assets/capital of the company are being used to generate profit. Furthermore, the result can be compared with that of investing the same capital in other ways. For example, what profit would arise as interest if the capital were left on deposit in the bank?

In some companies, monthly or quarterly results are expressed on a ROCE basis by 'annualizing' the profit results according to the number of calendar days in the period. The optimum ROA or ROCE result is achieved by keeping profit as high as possible, whilst maintaining assets at as low a level as possible.

19.3 Growth indices

The problem with using ROA or ROCE measures in isolation, as you may have realized, is that a very good result on this basis could be achieved through running down the business. That is, by *not* reinvesting in the business, and selling some of the assets each year at a profit, a good ratio could be achieved in the short term. In order to prevent this, a company's ROCE target is often accompanied by a growth target for either profit or, even better, revenue (sales). This growth target has a dual purpose, because not only is growth a good idea, but in the current economic climate, a company has to grow by at least the current rate of inflation to stand still. A growth target for the management of a company might be set at inflation plus 5 per cent, for example, in order to meet inflation and then demonstrate extra growth, that is, show *real* growth.

The growth indices are calculated as follows:

$$\text{Profit index} = \frac{\text{Profit (this year)}}{\text{Profit (last year)}}$$

$$\text{Sales index} = \frac{\text{Sales (this year)}}{\text{Sales (last year)}}$$

The sales index shows the rate at which the company *as a whole* is growing. The profit index not only shows how profit is growing but, when compared with the sales index, indicates how well the company is matching costs to revenue. For example, if sales are growing at 15 per cent per annum but profit only at 5 per cent, costs are growing at a faster rate than 15 per cent. Conversely if sales are growing at 5 per cent per annum and profit at 15 per cent, costs are being contained, and are growing at a much lower rate than sales, or even declining.

On an individual basis, most of us are concerned with the growth of our personal income. We like to see the growth in our pay exceed the rate of inflation, whether it be through an annual pay award or promotion. In other words, we are usually concerned with *absolute profit* and the *rate of profit growth*.

19.4 Net profit percentage or return on sales (ROS)

Another way in which profit is considered is as *net profit percentage* or *return on sales* (*ROS*). The equation for this is:

$$\text{Net profit percentage} = \frac{\text{Profit}}{\text{Sales}}$$

Again, as the name suggests, this figure is normally expressed as a percentage of profit on sales. The advantage of this measure is that it is more easily applied by product than ROCE, as the revenue per product is usually more readily available than assets per product in a multi-product factory. The allocation of assets by product is often difficult to achieve with any accuracy.

Ratios can also be calculated to measure labour efficiency, capacity usage and so on. Whereas the target ROCE figure can easily be determined by outside comparison, the ROS figure will vary considerably by product and industry because of market forces and the potential for *asset* or *capital turnover*.

19.5 Asset or capital turnover

Asset or *capital turnover* may be defined as the number obtained by dividing the annual sales value by the asset or capital value. It therefore represents the revenue-generating potential of the capital or assets:

$$\text{Asset/capital turnover} = \frac{\text{Sales}}{\text{Capital or assets}}$$

Example

A company in the food retailing industry, such as Sainsbury's or Tesco may have a profit percentage result of 4 per cent — a profit of 4p per pound of sales. This may appear low. However, the company's annual sales figure is likely to be in the region of five times the total value of capital invested (it has a capital turnover of five). As capital turnover multiplied by profit percentage equals ROA (see below), this produces a ROCE figure of four multiplied by five = 20 per cent.

The results in summary are:

- Profit percentage = 4 per cent
- Capital turnover = 5
- ROCE = 20%

Compare this with a high technology engineering company with a heavy investment in assets (as fixed assets, stocks and work in progress), for which the following results have arisen:

- Profit percentage = 10 per cent
- Capital turnover = 1.5
- ROCE = 10 × 1.5 = 15%

The engineering company has much better unit profitability, in terms of *profit* percentage, but presents a worse picture in terms of overall return on capital (ROCE) and capital turnover. In other words, it makes 10p in the pound in terms of profit on unit sales (which is better than the food company's 4p in the pound). But as the total sales value is only 1.5 times the capital invested (compared with the food company at 5 times), the return on capital only works out at 15 per cent compared with the food company's 20 per cent. That is, for every pound invested, the engineering company makes 15p and the food company 20p.

In summary, in a given period, it is possible to make more profit in a low profit margin/high turnover business than in a high margin/low volume business.

19.6 Cash limits

The final measure we will look at in this section is *cash limits*. The reason our measure of cash is expressed in this way is that in the normal course of business, a company has to operate within a cash limit. In other words, the company will have an agreed overdraft limit with its parent company or bank (depending on the source of cash funding). This limit will form a boundary within which the company will operate its cash management. Although this measure is placed last, it is by no means the least. Companies usually fail because they cannot pay their bills. In other words, they have exceeded their cash borrowing limits. We will deal with cash management in much more detail in Chapter 21.

Most of us are familiar, on a personal basis, with the problems of operating within cash limits!

19.7 The relationship between some of the key measures

Having reviewed the key management measures it is worth spending a little time establishing the relationship between the measures.

Figure 16: The relationship between some of the key measures

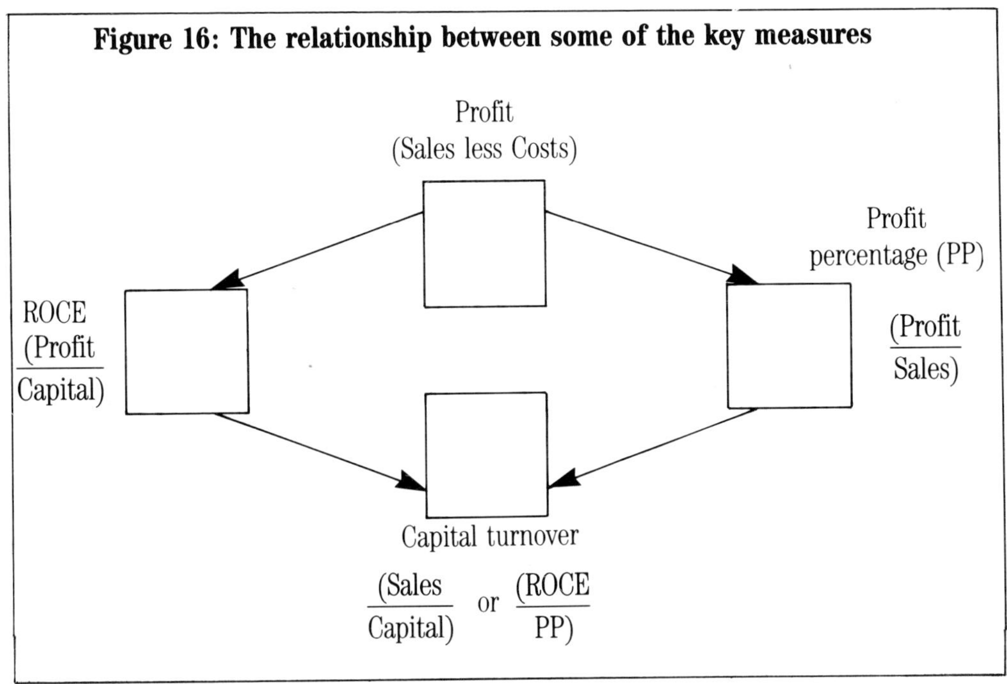

Summary

We can see from these relationships that they are all built up from sales, capital or assets, and costs, all other figures being an outcome of these. Our tasks in business can be summarized as:

- to grow sales revenue
- control costs
- manage assets and cash.

The next two chapters are devoted to investigating techniques used in managing these tasks.

Note that the measures used here are those used mainly by internal management — other factors are used by external reviewers. These are dealt with in the later chapters.

Exercise 17

The results of companies A and B were as follows for the last operating year:

	A	*B*
	£'000	*£'000*
Sales	350	600
Costs	315	573
Average capital employed	250	150

Calculate the profit, ROCE, net profit percentage and capital turnover for each company.

	A	*B*
(a) Profit (Sales less costs)	£	£
(b) ROCE (profit/capital × 100)	%	%
(c) Net profit percentage (profit/sales × 100)	%	%
(d) Capital turnover (sales/capital)	times	times

CHAPTER 20

Managing investment

This chapter explains the need for asset management and reviews the methods which can be used in evaluating investment decisions.

20.1 Why is it necessary to manage fixed assets?

We have seen previously that one of our key priorities in business is the control of assets. Fixed assets form a major part of the total business assets of most business.

In order to maintain a healthy return on assets (ROA), these fixed assets must be used to produce or operate in the most efficient way possible. Thus management must be actively involved in the maintenance and utilization of assets. Furthermore, because investment in fixed assets is often a long-term commitment, involving large sums of money, new capital expenditure must be rigorously reviewed. If we take the purchase of a new car as an example of investment in personal assets, we know that we will take many factors into consideration before buying. We will attempt to forecast the 'return' on our investment in terms of a series of factors, which will include:

- reliability
- ability to perform as required (acceleration, etc.)
- comfort
- economy (petrol, insurance and maintenance costs)
- value of investment (expected resale value)
- price (and trade-in offer)
- financing options (buy or lease).

The short-listed car models can then be measured against these factors to produce an optimum choice. Obviously in many cases this not done as a formal, written evaluation, but as a mental exercise. Nevertheless, the idea is still to make the best purchase, providing, of course, that it appears to be better value than our existing car.

We take this kind of care in making the purchase because we know the car is going to have to last several years, and that it will be expensive to change models in the short-term if we make the wrong decision.

Once we have purchased our new car, we will maintain it in good condition so that it both gives us proper usage and retains a high value.

Investment in company assets is done on very much the same basis, only the stakes are higher! That is, the investment is normally larger, the time period longer and mistakes more expensive. For instance, a company may spend £2 million on a new product factory which is designed to be economic over ten years. If the product becomes obsolete after only two years, substantial losses will be incurred. Managers therefore spend a considerable amount of time evaluating capital expenditure proposals prior to making decisions that commit the company to long-term and expensive investment. The rest of this chapter is concerned with the techniques used to assist in the evaluation process.

These investment decisions rely heavily on assumptions of future events. When we are planning new products or factories, we have to look ahead to company growth five, ten and even fifteen years ahead. The objectives for the business, as determined in the long-term plan, play an important part in this respect. Remember that time also plays an important part in the likelihood of future profits materializing. In other words, the further away in time a return is expected to arise, the greater the level of uncertainty that exists. This uncertainty has to be reflected in analysis of projects.

20.2 The need to manage risk and return

If a company has a return on asset or ROA target of 15 per cent, managers are unlikely to be interested in projects that yield less than this. In such a case, a *minimum* target of 15 per cent ROA will be set.

In the same way if we have a building society account which pays 9 per cent after tax, we will be unlikely to want to invest large sums of money at a lower rate.

The reason why a minimum is necessary is that some capital will be invested in areas which give no identifiable financial return. Investment in safety and employee benefits, such as the provision of fire fighting equipment or company sports facilities, are typical examples. Other investments will have to give a greater than target return to compensate for these investments.

In setting ROA targets, managers also have to consider risk — higher target returns may be demanded for higher risk investments. If we consider some of the capital expenditure decisions typically made, we can grade them by risk factor.

Capital expenditure	*Risk rating*
● cost-saving investments on existing processes	Low ↑
● Lease/buy decisions	
● Replacement machinery	
● Additional capacity	
● Marketing a product overseas	↓ High

20.3 Capital appraisal methods

In order to be effective, capital appraisal methods need to be capable of:

- ranking alternative proposals
- checking that investments will achieve at least the minimum target rate of return.

The sophistication of the method used also needs to be matched to the scale of the project being appraised in terms of risk and investment required. For example. a new factory proposal will require a more sophisticated analysis than a requisition for a replacement typewriter. In the end, both will need to satisfy the company's capital expenditure objectives although the scale of risk with each is very different.

For this reason, authority for approval of capital expenditure is often delegated to departmental managers. Each manager will then be able to approve capital expenditure that meets agreed company standards, up to a pre-set authority limit. In this way, only the large and risky projects will require top management attention and approval.

The main methods for capital expenditure appraisal are:

- The return on investment (ROI) method
- The pay-back method
- Discounted cash flow (DCF)
  - ★ The net present value method (NPV)
  - ★ The internal rate of return method (IRR).

These methods have one major factor in common — each requires the estimation of future benefits (in most cases, as cash flows).

In measuring most cash flows, it is easy to calculate the initial cash outflow (the investment). It is often more difficult to assess the subsequent incremental profits or cash inflows, particularly in the case of projects such as the launch of a new product which may have complex effects on existing products.

The level of uncertainty of future cash flows can be assessed to some extent using sensitivity analysis (which was described in Chapter 17). The level of project risk can be quantified using statistical probability techniques.

In the next pages, we will examine the project appraisal methods in more detail. Some of the methods involve quite complex equations and calculations. It is more important that you understand the reasoning behind each method — what each method is attempting to portray and when it should be used — rather than be able to calculate the results yourself.

Return on investment methods (ROI)
The ROI method is basically the same as the return on capital calculation we saw earlier. Unfortunately, there are several different calculation methods used. The most common are based on average profits and investment, or total profit and investment, as shown in the following equations:

$$\text{ROI} = \frac{\text{Estimated average profits}}{\text{Estimated average investment}} \times \frac{100}{1}$$

$$\text{ROI} = \frac{\text{Estimated total profits}}{\text{Forecast total investment}} \times \frac{100}{1}$$

There are arguments for and against these different definitions, but the most important factor is that, within a company, a standard definition is set and used. Let us now look at the use of this equation in a typical business situation.

Example

A factory manager is considering the purchase of a new packing machine and has two alternatives, for which he has the following data:

	Machine A	*Machine B*
Initial cost	£20,000	£20,000
Estimated life	4 years	4 years
Value at the end of life	£4,000	£6,000
Estimated future profits (before depreciation)		
Year 1	£10,000	£4,000
2	£10,000	£6,000
3	£6,000	£10,000
4	£2,000	£10,000
Total estimated profits	£28,000	£30,000

Which would be the better purchase, based upon return on investment? The answer is calculated as follows:

Step 1: Calculate average profits

	Machine A	*Machine B*
	£	£
Total additional profit	28,000	30,000
Less: Depreciation*	16,000	14,000
Total net profit	12,000	16,000
Divide by 4 to give average profits (over 4 years)	3,000	4,000

Step 2: Calculate average investment

	Machine A	*Machine B*
	£	£
Initial investment	20,000	20,000
Add: Residual value	4,000	6,000
	24,000	26,000
Divide by 2 to give average value of investment	12,000	13,000

*Depreciation amount is calculated as cost less residual value.

Step 3: Calculate ROI

	Machine A	*Machine B*
The return on investment is:	£3,000 × 100	£4,000 × 100
(using the average method)	£12,000	£13,000
	25%	31%

Machine B therefore gives the better rate of return.

Using the alternative 'total' calculation basis, the answers become:

	Machine A	*Machine B*
Initial investment	£20,000	£20,000
Profit after depreciation (see above)	£12,000	£16,000
ROI =	£12,000 / £20,000	£16,000 / £20,000
	60%	80%

Machine B also produces a better return on this basis.

Return on investment is a reflection of profitability and takes no account of the time element. You may have noticed that, in the above example, Machine A produces a much quicker cash return, which may be a much more important factor.

The payback method

The payback method uses cash as a basis. As its name suggests, it is used to calculate the period taken to pay back or recover the initial investment. The time taken for simple payback is a common criterion for approval used by companies. In other words, if the project does not pay for itself within a given period, say three years, the project is not approved.

Using the figures given above, it can be seen that machine A pays back the initial £20,000 investment in two years, whereas machine B takes three (see calculation below). On this basis, therefore, machine A is the better purchase. (We have assumed that profit before depreciation equals cash flow in.)

Payback calculation

	Machine A	*Machine B*
Initial investment	£20,000	£20,000
Less: Payback year 1	£10,000	£4,000
Balance at end of year 1	£10,000	£16,000
Less: Payback year 2	£10,000	£6,000
Balance at end of year 2	nil	£10,000
Less: Payback year 3		£10,000
Balance at end of year 3		nil

Note
Payback is ignored once the investment is paid back.

The major problem with this method is that it takes no account of cash flows beyond the payback period. Looking at our example again, if the cash return on machine A stopped after year 2, it would make no difference to the payback period. However the total cash return for machine A would now be £20,000, compared with £30,000 for machine B. Machine B would provide a better return in the long term.

Discounted cash flow method
Discounted cash flow (DCF) is a method of capital investment appraisal which not only takes into acount the overall profitability of projects, but also allows for the timing of cash returns and outflows. It therefore combines the benefits of the two previous methods.

The principle behind DCF is that cash held now is of greater value than the same amount of cash received in the future. In addition, the longer the time before the cash is received the less value it has. All the future incremental cash flows generated by the project are estimated both in terms of their value and when they will occur. Discounting is then applied to them in order to take the timing into account.

Discounting is the same as the compound effect of interest but in reverse. If, for example, we invest £100 for three years at 10 per cent annual compound, after three years we would receive:

Year 1 £100 × 1.1 = £110
Year 2 £110 × 1.1 = £121
Year 3 £121 × 1.1 = £133.10

On a discounted basis, therefore, if our target rate of return is 10 per cent, £133.10 received in three years' time (at a rate of 10 per cent) is £100.

As you can see, this reflects the fact that an amount of cash to be received in the future is worth less and less in today's terms the longer it takes to materialize. This is because when discounting a future cash receipt we must reflect both *inflation* and *uncertainty*.

Net present value (NPV)
The present value method reduces all future cash flows to current values.

The formula for this is:

$$P = \frac{S}{(1+r)^n}$$

Where: P is the present value.
S is the future sum received.
r is the rate of interest expressed as a proportion (e.g. 10% = 0.1).
n is the number of years hence at which S is received.

In real life, the timing of future cash flow is complex, particularly when items such as tax payments are taken into account (capital allowance reliefs may have a big impact on company taxation). Some assumptions are normally made to ease the calculation. For example, initial capital expenditure is assumed to occur at year zero.

If we stay with our previous simple example, we are now informed that we will only invest in machine A or B, providing the chosen machine gives a better return than investing the capital in securities (with a current interest forecast of 15 per cent). Using the net present value method we get the following results:

Machine A

Year	*Net cash flow* £	*Discount factor* £	*NPV* £
0	(20,000)	nil	(20,000)
1	10,000	$\frac{1}{1.15}$	8,696
2	10,000	$\frac{1}{(1.15)^2}$	7,561
3	6,000	$\frac{1}{(1.15)^3}$	3,945
4	2,000+4,000*	$\frac{1}{(1.15)^4}$	3,431
		NPV =	+3,633

*Assumes receipt of scrap value at end of year 4.

Note that the initial investment is shown as a negative cash flow in year 0.

As the comparative net present value of investing the capital at 15 per cent is zero, the rate of return of machine A is well in excess of this. Similarly, the NPV of machine B is +3737, which is close to that of machine A, and also well in excess of 15 per cent.

In order to short cut the calculation of these factors, tables are used which give the standard discount factors for NPV by discount rate percentage.

Internal rate of return (IRR)

The NPV method determines whether our investment earns more (positive NPV) or less (negative NPV) than our target rate of return. The IRR method, on the other hand, determines the rate of interest at which the NPV is zero — the earning rate of the investment. The most common way of finding the IRR is by trial and error, using different percentage return/NPV tables to narrow down the percentage through alternate positive and negative NPVs until one approximating to zero is achieved.

Example

IRR for machine A

Year	*Cash flow* £	*24% factor*	*Present value* £	*25% factor*	*Present value* £
0	(20,000)	1	(20,000)	1	(20,000)
1	10,000	0.8065	8,065	0.8000	8,000
2	10,000	0.6504	6,504	0.6400	6,400
3	6,000	0.5245	3,147	0.5120	3,072
4	6,000	0.4230	2,538	0.4096	2,458
Totals	12,000		+ 254		− 70

For machine A, the IRR is between 24 per cent and 25 per cent. To be more exact it approximates to:

$$24 + \frac{254}{324} = \underline{\underline{24.8\%}}$$

Note that the 324 used in the equation above is the difference between the cash flow results at the two rates (+254 to −70).

IRR for machine B

Year	*Cash flow* £	*21% factor*	*Present value* £	*23% factor*	*Present value* £
0	(20,000)	1	(20,000)	1	(20,000)
1	4,000	0.8264	3,306	0.8130	3,252
2	6,000	0.6830	4,098	0.6610	3,966
3	10,000	0.5645	5,645	0.5374	5,374
4	16,000	0.4665	7,464	0.4369	6.990
Totals	16,000		+ 513		− 418

We now know that the IRR for machine B is between 21 per cent and 23 per cent. A more exact answer can be calculated from the results on the table as follows:

$$21 + 2 \times \frac{513}{931} = \underline{\underline{21.1\%}}$$

Note, as in the previous calculation, 931 is equal to the difference between +513 and −418.

Summary of results

To compare the results produced by the various methods, the results are tabulated below. The better result in each case is shown in heavy type.

	Machine A	*Machine B*
Simple ROI (average basis)	25%	**31%**
Payback	**2 years**	3 years
NPV	**>15%**	**>15%**
IRR	**24.8%**	22.1%

As you can see, from our initial method, machine B *appears* to be a better buy but once the timing of return on investment is taken into account, machine A, with its higher value returns in the early years, is shown to be the better buy.

As mentioned at the start of these calculations, it is not essential for a manager to know how to calculate DCF results — there are normally specialists available to do this. However, it is important to understand what the various methods of investment appraisal represent, and why companies have return on investment targets.

Exercise 18

There are several ways of assessing the value of an investment. Match the methods shown with the descriptions given below.

Methods	*Description*
(1) Simple cash flow	______
(2) Discounted cash flow (DCF)	______
(3) Payback	______
(4) Return on investment	______
(5) Internal rate of return (IRR)	______
(6) Net present value (NPV)	______

Description

(a) The return on the project expressed as a return on capital percentage after taking time of return into account.

(b) The method of adjusting cash flows to take into account the effect of the passage of time.

(c) The measurement of cash spent versus total cash returns.

(d) The method of calculating and displaying 'returns' to give present time equivalent values.

(e) The simple method of displaying profit or 'return' in relation to investment.

(f) The method showing the recovery of the original cash investment.

CHAPTER 21

The management of working capital

This chapter shows the need for working capital management and illustrates techniques that can be used to manage current assets more effectively.

21.1 The need for working capital management

The working capital of a company is the investment made in current assets. Compared with fixed assets, which represent long-term investments needing careful assessment prior to purchase, current assets tend to be much more short term and volatile. Because of this, current assets both need, and respond to, professional management on a day-to-day basis. Indeed, many new and growing companies have folded because of *over-trading*.

Over-trading happens when a company grows quickly and is unable to fund its working capital requirements from its cash resources. In other words, the need for working capital has got out of control.

A company's working capital will be invested in current assets of the following major categories:

	Stocks and Work in Progress
+	Debtors
+	Cash
=	Current assets
−	Current liabilities
=	Net current assets

In the remainder of the chapter we will deal with the control and management of each category in turn, starting with stocks and work in progress.

21.2 Managing stocks and work in progress

When measured against a yardstick such as total assets, or revenue, the values of stocks and work in progress vary considerably from company to company and from industry to industry. In the aerospace industry, for example, a single product may take years to make and involve a considerable investment in both stocks and work in progress. Conversely, in a labour-intensive industry, or a consumer product industry such as bakeries, work in progress will be negligible and material stocks relatively low.

Industrial manufacturing and engineering companies are particularly concerned with stock control, having such large and complex inventories to control. Lucas Industries have stocks of some £300 million, which represent approximately 30 per cent of gross assets.

Let us now look at the factors influencing stock holding.

Why should we keep stock values low?
We saw earlier that we can improve our ROA by keeping the total of assets as low as possible. This is the first reason why we need to control our stocks and work in progress (otherwise known as *inventories*), but there are also other reasons:

- To reduce the additional costs associated with the storage and handling of excessive stocks, in terms of extra manpower, premises costs, insurance, etc.
- To minimize the chance of deterioration and wastage through:

  - ★ physical deterioration through age or damage
  - ★ technical obsolescence caused by the part or product having been superseded

- Finally, to free cash to be invested more profitably elsewhere.

Why should we keep stock values high?
There are, however, good reasons why we should maintain high levels of stock.

- Materials and parts can be purchased more cheaply in large quantities.
- Reserve or buffer stocks may be used to smooth production, thereby overcoming delivery problems, or industrial relations stoppages at other manufacturing stages.
- Sufficient stocks of finished goods should be held to enable prompt and efficient delivery to the customer. The level will of course vary by product and industry (the strategic stocks of coal held at power stations is an extreme case).
- Finished goods stockholdings should be sufficient to deal with seasonal fluctuations and the variations in ordering patterns. For instance, the car industry in the UK has to build stock to cope with the new registration sales peak each August.
- Economies of scale in multi-product production lines mean that once a line is set up for a particular product, economic volumes are produced. Sometimes this will mean 'making for stock', there being a low level of current orders for the product.

In each company these opposing factors, which cause stock to increase or decrease, have to be balanced out and an *ideal* stock level determined. However, before we consider how to set ideal stock levels, we should look at the types of stock in more detail.

The current trend towards 'just-in-time' manufacturing has led to stock reductions in many manufacturing companies. This is explained in detail in the next section.

21.3 Types of stock

Raw materials, parts and components
The first inventory stage consists of raw materials, parts and components awaiting issue to the manufacturing process. The stock holding policy in this area has been the subject of much discussion in recent years, with particular attention being paid to Japanese flow-line production policies, or 'just-in-time' manufacturing.

These Japanese policies require the suppliers of parts and components to hold the stock themselves, and make deliveries direct to the production line of the main manufacturer at predetermined times. This, of course puts the onus of stock-holding on to the component manufacturer, and he, presumably, requires some financial compensation in terms of piece-part price. It also requires accurate production planning by the controllers of the main production process, and smooth production flow.

In planning the inventory of purchased goods, the potential savings made by tight control of stock holdings have to be balanced against:

- the cost of potential interruptions to production
- the optimum use of purchasing power by, say, advance purchasing, to avoid anticipated increases in material prices, which could be due to:
  - ★ natural price fluctuations in raw material commodities, such as copper and lead
  - ★ currency movements on imports
  - ★ an imminent price increase by the supplier.

Alternatively, to take advantage of the bulk discounts available on quantity purchase, phased delivery agreements will accompany such an agreement so that they do not necessarily lead to high stock holdings. Phased delivery may well suit both purchaser and vendor.

In summary, company policy on raw materials, parts and component stocks must be flexible enough to enable the purchasing department to exploit price opportunities, while at the same time taking the costs penalties incurred through holding excess stocks into account.

Work in progress (WIP)

In a typical manufacturing company, materials and parts pass through a number of processes before finally emerging as finished products. At each stage the materials add value, with the direct and indirect costs. The time required for each process adds to the value of work in progress. Moreover, the need for smooth production may lead to the creation of buffer stocks. Once again, the cost of maintaining these buffer stocks has to be matched against penalties of lost production.

In some industries, particularly those involved in long-term projects, such as construction and heavy plant manufacture, it may be possible to reduce the burden on the manufacturers of maintaining buffer stocks by getting the customer to fund part of the cost through pre-payments. This should be explored as an option in all cases of large individual orders with long production cycles.

Finished goods stock

The stocks of finished goods held by a company will vary by product and industry. By and large, the greater the product value, or the more specialized it is, the less chance there is that the finished product will be immediately available.

To take an example, even in the retail trade, where stock availability is paramount, more expensive items such as furniture may well still be subject to delivery delay. Compare this with food items such as baked beans, for which no sales would occur unless the product were immediately available.

In determining its finished goods stock policy, a company must balance the needs of the customer against the cost of holding stock. It is obviously not good business sense to hold large stocks of high-value specialized engineering plant. Whilst, ideally, a customer might like to buy such plant 'off the shelf', he will normally expect to commission it for later delivery. However, if a company has a contract to supply components to a major manufacturer, it would be prudent to hold sufficient stocks to ensure good and constant customer service.

21.4 Setting ideal stock levels and controlling lead times

In order to minimize stock holdings of purchased materials, the company must consider:

- the cost of processing and handling orders together with the cost of holding stock
- the risk factors associated with various levels of stock holding
- the consequences of a 'stock-out' position.

Much statistical work has been done in this area and mathematical models for stock control have been produced. Many of these models are now available as computerized stock control systems. They have features such as automatic re-ordering (see under 'Lead times' below), triggered when a low stock limit is reached.

Many of these systems also include the standard formula that is used in calculating *economic order quantities* — optimum order size — balancing the cost of handling orders against the cost of holding large stocks. The formula is:

$$\text{EOQ} = \sqrt{\frac{2cd}{h}}$$

In which:

c = the ordering/handling cost per unit
d = annual rate of demand or usage
h = annual holding cost per unit.

The effect of this formula is shown by the following graph.

Figure 17: Economic order quantity graph

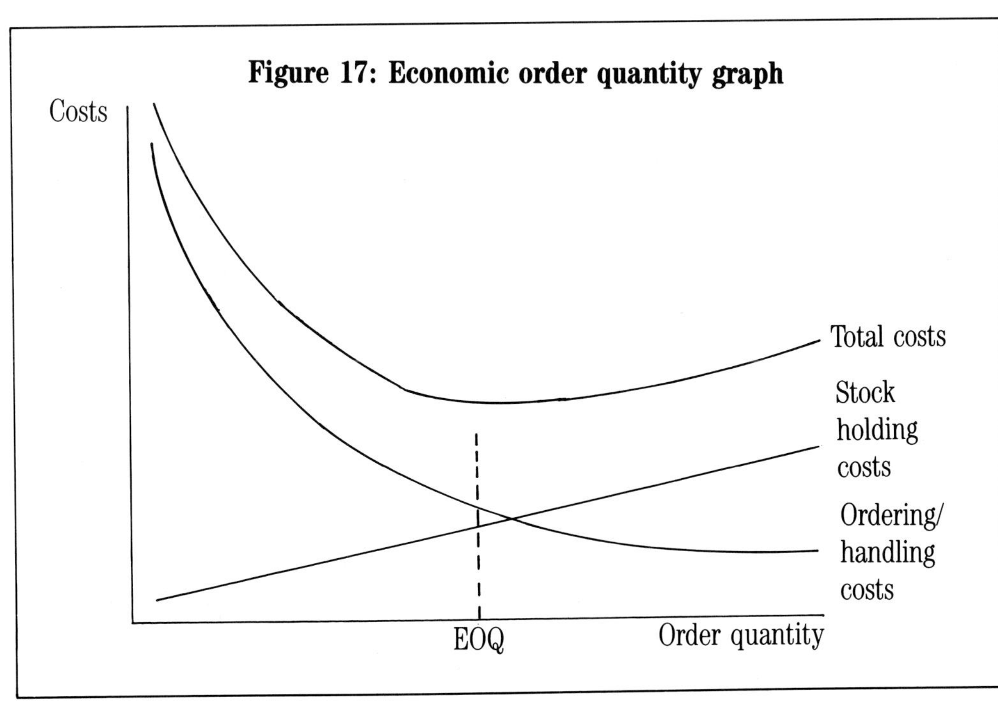

You should be able to see from this graph how ordering/handling costs per unit go down as the order quantity rises, whereas unit stock-holding costs increase with stock levels and holding times. When the two are added together the lowest combined total (the lowest point on the total cost line) gives us the EOQ.

Exercise 19

A manufacturing plant uses 1,000 tons of steel per month. It is estimated that it costs £3 per year to keep a ton of steel in stock, and each order costs £20 per ton in handling costs. Calculate the economic order quantity using the standard formula which is repeated below.

First complete the following table:

c = the ordering cost per unit =
d = annual rate of demand or usage =
h = annual holding cost per unit =

Now use these numbers to complete the equation below:

$$\text{EOQ} = \sqrt{\frac{2cd}{h}} = \sqrt{\frac{2\times \quad \times \quad}{\quad}} = \underline{\underline{\qquad\qquad}} \text{ tons}$$

Lead times

In addition to considering how much to order, it is necessary to consider *when* to place the order. Order lead times will depend on the average delay between placing orders and receiving the goods, and the need for buffer stocks. The level of buffer stock can be determined by matching stock-holding costs against the consequence of a stock-out position. There are formulae and equations available which are designed to produce optimum purchasing timings.

In some companies, sophisticated computerized stock and re-order programmes are installed. These automatically raise orders when the lower stock limit is reached. This limit is calculated to be equivalent to the usage during re-ordering lead time plus a safety margin. For these systems to operate effectively they must be well managed. This requires the system to be:

- set up correctly
- kept up to date with stock movements
- adjusted for any part re-specifications.

21.5 Stock valuation

As mentioned previously, a product changes in value whilst going through its manufacturing stages. When we want to value stocks and work in progress at a given point in time, we need to attribute values to each product at its current process stage. The diagram below shows how value gets added to a product in a two stage production process. At the bottom of the diagram, the various methods of stock valuation used at each stage are listed.

Figure 18: Stock valuation diagram

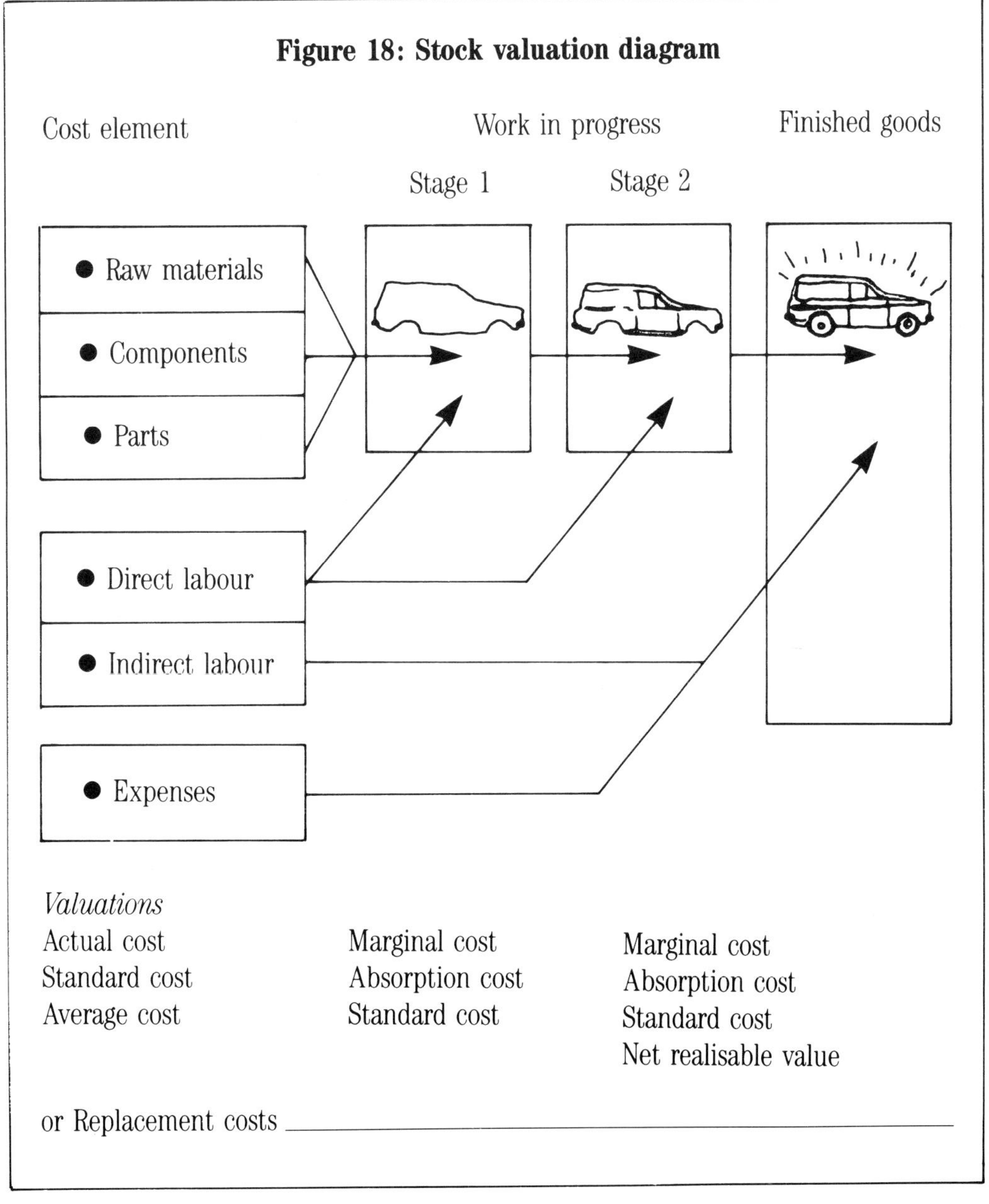

The detailed definitions of these valuation methods are:

- *Actual costs* The use of actual cost may seem the obvious way to value stock. However, the stock of a particular material or component at a given time often includes items from a mixture of deliveries, at different actual costs. Typically, the way actual cost is worked out is the net amount remaining from a series of purchases less issues to production. The purchases may well have been made at differing unit prices and issues taken out of general stock and not from a specific purchase batch.

  In order to cope with this situation, accountants value both stock and issues, using one of a series of assumptions, the most popular being: *FIFO* (*first in, first out*), where it is assumed that the oldest stock is issued first, or *LIFO* (*last in, first out*), where the assumption is made that the most recent stock is issued first.

  LIFO, however, is not generally accepted as a suitable method of stock valuation because it neither reflects normal practice nor gives an accurate profit and loss charge.
- *Average costs and standard costs* A simpler method than FIFO or LIFO is often to use average costs (the average cost of purchase) or standard costs in cases where an up-to-date standard costing system is installed. The advantage of standard costing is that it can apply to all stages in the production process.
- *Marginal costs or absorption costs* These terms refer to the actual basis of valuation. Stocks valued on a marginal basis will only have direct costs applied, whereas those on an absorption basis will contain an allocation of overheads.
- *Net realizable value* This is a method of valuing finished goods stocks at the price they would realize if sold, less any costs of realization (sales, marketing, distribution, etc.).
- *Replacement cost* This, as its name suggests, is a method of valuation that involves assessing the value of stock according to the cost of replacement or *current cost*. This is often used for insurance purposes.

21.6 Stock control and turnover

In this chapter we have briefly looked at stock management, valuation and control. It *is* a brief look, as stock control techniques are highly sophisticated these days, with many different computerized stock control systems available.

Nevertheless, although the systems may be computerized, the management of stock still has a large human content, in terms of controlling the parameters of the system, stock value maintenance, introducing new items, removing old stock and so on.

It is also worth remembering that stock values usually follow a normal distribution pattern, with a small number of stock lines having the bulk of the total value. The

'80:20' rule (or Pareto law) often holds true, with 20 per cent of the stock representing 80 per cent of its value. Priority should therefore be given to controlling high value items.

Finally, a crude measure of the control of stocks is provided by measuring *stock turnover*. This can be done in two ways, the first being a comparison of total stock with annual sales. Alternatively, a better measure, as it relates more closely to stock holding, is to compare the stock and work in progress values with the annual cost of goods sold.

For internal purposes, instead of using annual figures for sales or cost of sales, it is common to use the figures for the previous quarter on an annualized basis, as a substitute for the annual figures.

The equations on this basis are:

$$\textit{Stock turnover} = \frac{\text{3 month's sales} \times 4}{\text{Total stocks}}$$

$$= \frac{\text{3 month's COS} \times 4}{\text{Total stocks}}$$

When the result is multiplied by 4 it gives an annual equivalent of the number of times that stock is turned over in a year.

Alternatively, the figures above can be converted into the number of working revenue days that the stock value represents. Working days are used instead of calendar days, to represent the number of days of operational activity that is represented by the stock.

Exercise 20

List three reasons why stock values should be low.

(1) ____________________

(2) ____________________

(3) ____________________

List three reasons why stock levels should be kept high.

(1) ____________________

(2) ____________________

(3) ____________________

21.7 Managing debtors

The other major area of business where funds are tied up is in debtors, that is, money owed by customers. Of course, in some businesses — such as retailing — the customer pays immediately. In industry, however, it is normal practice to invoice the customer (give him *credit*) and for the customer to pay the bill in due course.

At any one time there will always be a sum of money outstanding from customers representing invoices so far unpaid. The company's aim from a finance perspective should be to keep this figure as low as possible. However, it should also be borne in mind that, from a sales viewpoint, the practice of giving credit provides a competitive advantage. If, therefore, we review a company with credit sales running at £1.2 million a year and with customers that take on average two months to pay, we can estimate the average total amount owed at any one time as follows:

$$\text{Debtors} = \frac{\text{Sales} \times \text{Average credit period (months)}}{12}$$

$$= \frac{\text{£}1.2 \text{ million} \times 2}{12} = \underline{\underline{\text{£}200{,}000}}$$

The average value of invoices outstanding, and, therefore, the current debt funding requirement, is £200,000.

Exercise 21

Z Industries PLC reported sales of approximately £1,400 million in the year ended December 31st 198X, and at that date had debtors to the value of £300 million.

Assuming all sales to be on a credit basis, calculate the *average* time taken to pay by customers. Use an adjusted version of the equation above, as follows:

$$\text{Average time to pay (in months)} = \frac{\text{Value of debt} \times 12}{\text{Annual sales value}}$$

$$= \frac{\boxed{} \times 12}{\boxed{}} = \underline{\underline{\boxed{}}} \text{ months}$$

21.8 How can debtors be controlled?

The value of debtors is determined by the volume of sales and the period of time it takes to collect amounts due. As we have already determined that we require sales growth, we obviously do not want to restrict this, except in one area. We do not want to grow *bad risk* business, or, in other words, sell on credit to customers who are unlikely to pay for the goods. *Credit checking* is therefore one factor we can use to slow the growth of debt.

The remaining areas for controlling debtors are all to do with the timely payment of invoices. The key factors affecting timely payment are:

- quality of the product and service
- Credit policy
  - ★ granting of credit
  - ★ credit period given
- quality of administration
  - ★ accurate recording of delivery quantity and 'proof'
  - ★ fast and accurate invoicing and statement production
  - ★ good customer query service
  - ★ responsive customer account status system
  - ★ well-defined slow payment follow-up
- good management control system.

Now let us consider these items in more detail:

The quality of goods and service
This may appear to be a strange item to head the list of factors affecting invoice payment, nevertheless it is one of the most important because dissatisfaction with the quality of the product, or the way in which the service was supplied is one of the main reasons for non-payment of invoices. Therefore, serving a customer efficiently and correctly at the first attempt leads to quicker payment. 'Get it right first time' is a slogan used internally to emphasize this aspect to employees.

Credit policy
A company needs policies on both the *granting* of credit and the credit *period* to be adopted. The latter should be part of the marketing strategy of the business, because long-term credit is a key selling tool which should be costed in the same way as other forms of sales promotion. In other words, the cost of giving credit should always be matched against the profitability of additional sales produced.

Longer credit periods are used in some industries to offset seasonal demand. For example, coal is produced all year round, but is consumed largely in winter months. Longer credit terms are amongst the inducements used to even up trade activity.

It has been known for companies to go the other way and offer very restricted credit terms, say seven day payment, but use the lower funding requirement to offer other benefits such as lower prices or discounts. By and large, in a competitive industrial environment extended credit can only be avoided by offering other inducements.

The policy on granting credit will vary from industry to industry. It is important for each company to appoint a manager responsible for granting credit. That responsibility should also be accompanied by the responsibility for bad debts — the associated control measure. The person responsible will normally be an accounting or sales manager. If the sales are few and long term, an accountant may be preferred. If the sales are many, widespread, and with fast delivery, it may be more practical for the salesman to arrange for credit to be given. If this is the case, a system for penalizing the salesman for bad debts needs to be in place to counteract the tendency to make sales at all costs.

Once it reaches a certain size, a company will normally introduce a formal customer vetting process. This will often involve using an agency specializing in providing credit information on potential customers, such as Dun and Bradstreet.

Quality of administration

By administration, we mean not only the administration department, but all persons involved in completing paperwork connected with the sale — salesmen, delivery drivers, etc. As we saw above in the section on product quality and service, the customer will pay more readily if the product and service match expectations.

Well-designed and correctly completed paperwork will ensure that the customer receives the right product, in the right quantities, on the right day. The customer should be requested to provide proper acknowledgement of delivery, so that delivery is proven. The invoice can confirm the correct product, quantity, order number and delivery at the agreed price.

Invoicing and statements

Another common reason for slow payment by the customer is slow production of invoices and statements. The customer cannot begin to process the invoice for payment until he has received it. In addition, the sooner the invoice is received after delivery, the less likely the chance of confusion with other deliveries.

Good customer query service

There is often a direct correlation between size of the outstanding debt and the number of unresolved customer queries. If a customer has a problem with a company, his only form of direct redress is not to pay his invoice, although his problem may not even be associated with the specific unpaid bill.

Many people telephoning a large company with a query will have experienced being passed around from extension to extension, with little hope of finding anyone who can deal with the query directly. Robert Townsend, in his book *Up the Organisation*, recommends that managers should telephone their own companies to find out how their staff react to queries.

Formal responsibility for recording and dealing with invoice queries in a timely way should be allocated. Proper analysis of customer queries also provides good free information on product or service problems.

Responsive customer account status system

A good customer query service will benefit considerably from knowing the status of a customer's account when answering queries. For example, if there is a problem with one of several outstanding invoices, the query clerk could agree a course of action to resolve the problem, and at the same time confirm immediate payment for the remaining outstanding bills. Terminal-based accounting systems can be extremely useful in this area.

Well-defined slow payment follow-up

As a rule, the longer an invoice is outstanding, the more difficult it is to obtain payment. Because of this, a company should establish a procedure for handling overdue payments. This should involve a sequence of letters, personal calls etc., and finally transfer to solicitors for collection. Again, a computerized system is of great assistance in monitoring this process, which must be systematically approached in order to be successful.

Priority should be given to the payment of large outstanding accounts as the '80:20' rule normally applies here. (This rule states that 80 per cent of value is normally accounted for by 20 per cent of the goods/services concerned.)

Good management control system
The overall control of debtors is achieved using several factors:

- The overall debtors are measured using *days' sales outstanding* (DSO), using a method similar to that used for stocks, but substituting days for months. The daily credit sales value for the last three months is divided into the debtors' value to give the equivalent number of days. These can then be reported on a monthly basis.
- The amount of invoicing outstanding, a measure of the invoicing efficiency, can be calculated using the *accrued* (i.e. uninvoiced) *revenue* and dividing that by the average daily sales value.
- The quality of outstanding debt can be assessed by ageing analysis. From this, rises in total debt can be evaluated to see if they are caused by new invoicing, or an accumulation of old outstanding amounts.

Computerized invoicing and debt control has helped this kind of analysis considerably by facilitating date sorting of outstanding invoices. A typical profile might be:

Ageing analysis of debtors

	£M	*%*
Debt outstanding:		
Up to 30 days	155	67
31-60 days old	60	26
61-90 days old	12	5
Over 90 days	5	2
Total	232	100
Average days' sales	£5M	
DSO	46.4	

In addition, as mentioned previously, analysis of numbers and types of queries can help in reducing causes of slow payment. The DSO (Days Sales Outstanding) figure of 46.4 days means that the value of debt is equivalent to 46.4 days of sales. From a management point of view it is important to know whether this figure is increasing or decreasing. The absolute figure could be reasonable for a company offering 30 days credit on normal accounts, however, the figure should be kept as small as possible. Similarly the ageing profile should be monitored and the older debt (say over 60 days) investigated specifically by accounts.

One technique of advancing cash payment is to give a discount for fast payment, for example, 2 per cent if paid within 7 days. The cost of a scheme such as this has to be compared with the cost of capital incurred without the discount.

You might have previously assumed that control of debtors was solely in the hands of the accountants. You should now realize that debt can be affected by all of us connected with the product or customer service.

21.9 Managing creditors

Creditors are the people to whom we owe money, whether they are the corner shop we owe for a week's supply of newspapers, or a shipbuilder we owe for a super-tanker we have bought.

In company accounts, the creditors total is deducted from the total of working capital to give net working capital. The main categories of creditor are:

- *Trade creditors* — payments outstanding on purchased goods and services
- *Taxation* — owed by the company such as payroll taxes and corporation tax
- *Payments in advance by customers* — we owe the customer until the product is delivered
- *Short-term bank loans* — monies owed to the banks against short term borrowings

To a certain extent, the payment of trade creditors may be used to balance very short-term cash flows. Some companies are notorious for slow payment of invoices, others such as Marks and Spencer pride themselves on fast payment.

Marks and Spencer pay promptly because they negotiate very keen prices with their suppliers, and if they combined this with slow payment they could bankrupt their suppliers. M&S are assisted, of course, by the fact that, as a retail business, they are paid instantly for their sales.

It is possible to use delaying tactics on creditors to a certain extent but it should be realized that slow payers will ultimately be charged higher prices by their suppliers to compensate for loss of bank interest.

21.10 Cash management

In company terms, 'cash' means actual cash held by the company (petty cash and so on), money in the bank and short-term investments (those which can be easily be converted into cash). Cash or treasury management is important for three main reasons:

- It is necessary for transaction purposes. In other words, a company must be able to meet everyday payments in the normal course of business to employees, creditors, the taxman, etc., as well as pay for fixed asset purchases.
- It is advisable for precautionary purposes, to hold a 'buffer' against unexpected cash needs.
- It is desirable for speculative purposes. Proper cash management involves making profit through taking advantages of 'bargains'. For example, a company involved in the purchase of commodity raw materials, such as lead for batteries, might well take advantage of a price fall to prepurchase large stocks. Similarly, any company involved in international trade needs to manage its foreign currency cash flows well in order to take advantage of

potentially favourable currency movements.

The ability to earn profit through longer term investments must be weighed against the need to hold cash. As most people know from personal cash management, the longer money is committed for investment, the greater the interest or return. For instance, compare the following examples:

- Current bank accounts, in exchange for flexibility of use, pay little or no interest.
- Bank deposit acounts and building society accounts pay interest on a scale which increases as the committed period gets longer and the minimum investment gets larger.

In the case of a company, we expect funding to be matched with investment. For example, we expect fixed assets to be purchased with long-term capital such as share capital. On the other hand, we expect short-term requirements such as seasonal stock building to be financed by short-term loans such as bank overdrafts. The way that a company's assets build up and are funded over time are shown in the graph below.

Figure 19: Graph showing the pattern of company funding over time

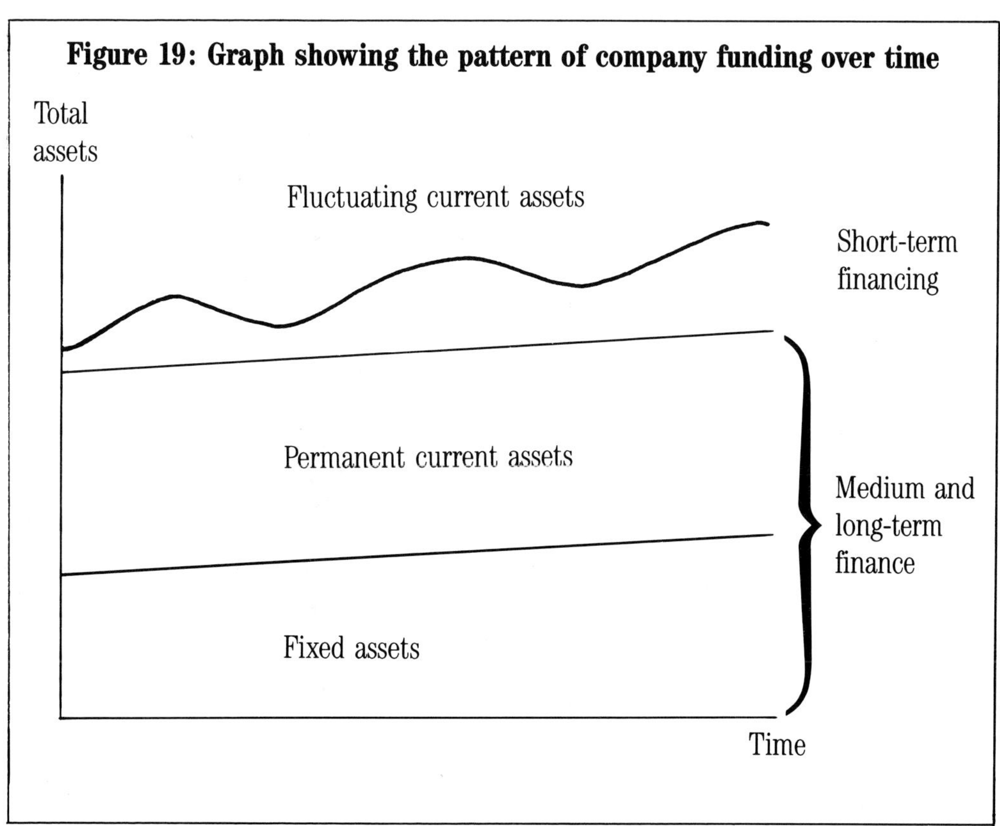

Fluctuations in current assets are caused by seasonal and trade sales patterns. For example, in the car industry, the August sales peak will involve a build up of stocks prior to this date, an increase in debtors as the sales are made, followed by a large cash inflow as the payments are made.

21.11 Funding new products and new projects

The funding of new products or processes also involves a time cycle effect. When a project is initiated, cash is invested in plant, equipment, salaries and wages, raw materials, WIP, finished goods stocks, debtors and so on. Until the first product is paid for, the cash flow is all one way — out.

One aspect of company cash management should be to ensure that enough funds are available to invest in modernization, new products, improved processes etc. The graph below shows a typical product life cycle. The aim of a company should be to have products at all stages of the cycle, with the more mature products funding the development of new ones.

Obviously, the more healthy products the company has, and the longer they stay in the mature cash-positive state, the better for that company. The only problem is that this situation encourages complacency, with the company being loath to invest in new ventures because of the success of existing products. Companies in this position can suddenly find their main products fade very quickly and they have no replacements available.

When developing new products, the initial time periods of negative cash flow may extend for years in the development of large products or processes such as aerospace projects. The management of cash over time is a crucial factor in the ultimate profitability of these projects.

Figure 20: Cash flows over a typical product life cycle

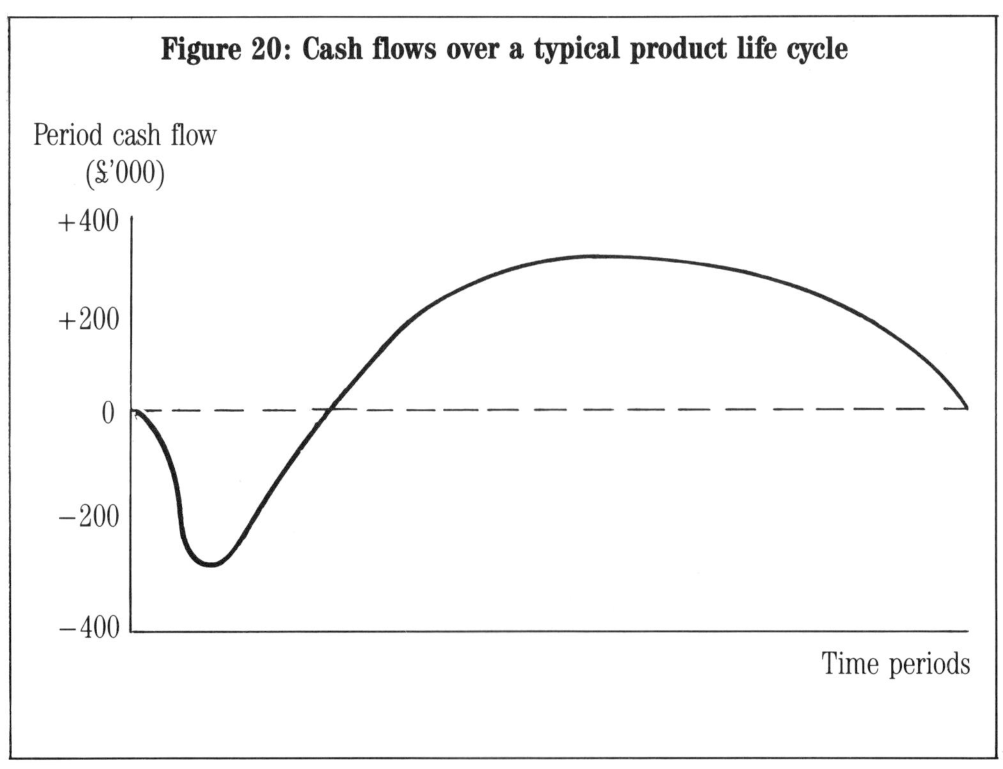

It is important to remember that there is a cost of holding cash, that is if cash which could otherwise be invested and be earning interest or profit is held it is costing the company money. So, in the same manner as previous assets, the cash balance should be as low as possible — providing, of course, that suitable investments exist.

21.12 Cash budgets and forecasts

We saw in Chapter 16 how annual cash budgets are produced. In order to keep cash under tight control, detailed monthly budgets may also be produced. In these, the amount and timing of each cash flow movement is forecast and monitored closely, in the same way as we might plot personal cash transactions. Creating monthly cash forecasts can prove a complex exercise as the following example illustrates.

Example

A company expects sales of £1,000,000 in January and £800,000 in February. Of these, 10 per cent are cash sales which are allowed 5 per cent discount. The rest are credit sales. Of the credit sales:

- 25 per cent are paid within 30 days, for which they receive 3 per cent discount
- 50 per cent are paid in the month following invoicing
- 24 per cent one month after that
- the remaining 1 per cent are bad debts.

If you have to prepare an estimate of cash receipts the answer would be:

Analysis of sales

	January £	*February* £
Total	1,000,000	800,000
(10% cash sales (excl. disc))	(100,000)	(80,000)
Credit sales	900,000	720,000
Sales receipts analysis:		
Received: Within 30 days (25%)	225,000	180,000
(3% discount)	(6,750)	(5,400)
	218,250	174,600
Following month (50%)	450,000	360,000
Month after that (24%)	216,000	172,800
Credit sales receipts	884,250	707,400
Cash sales	100,000	80,000
(5% cash discount)	5,000	4,000
Cash sales receipts	95,000	76,000
Note: Bad debts	9,000	7,200

Cash flow estimate

	January	*February*	*March*	*April*	*May*
Cash sales receipts (after discount)	95,000	76,000			
1 months' credit (less discount)		218,250	174,600		
2 months' credit			450,000	360,000	
3 months' credit				216,000	172,800
Total receipts	95,000	294,250	624,600	576,000	172,800

From this, which represents the estimate of two months' sales income only, you can see that cash planning is complex when done in detail, particularly when all the other items of expenditure are included, as shown in the diagram below.

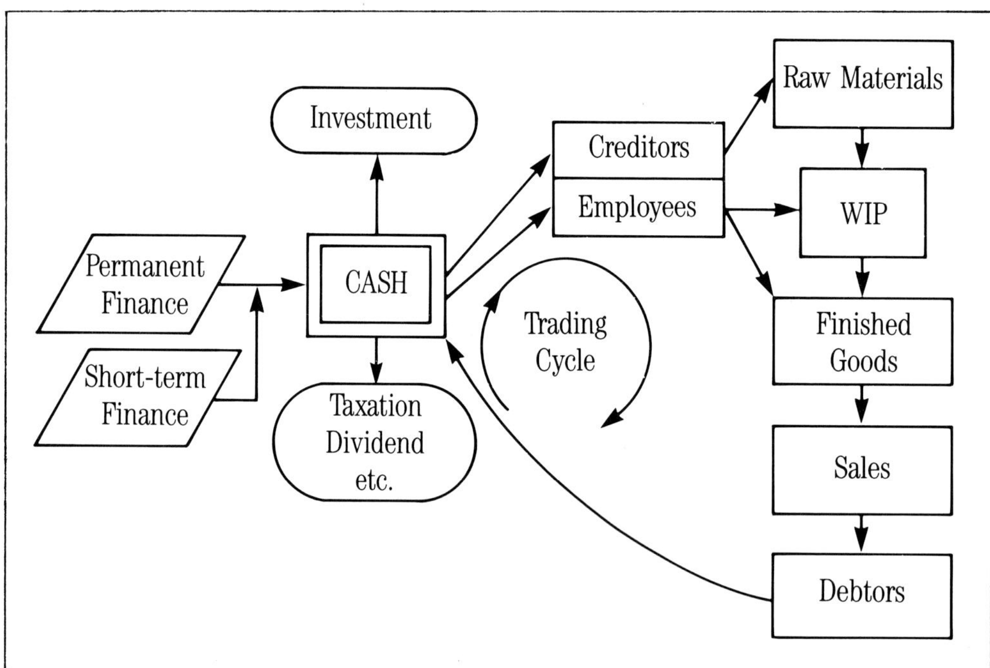

PART 5

Working with company results

CHAPTER 22

The annual report and accounts

This chapter describes the contents of the annual report and accounts document produced by companies. It also outlines some of the rules and conventions that have to be complied with in their preparation.

22.1 What reports do companies publish?

All limited companies are obliged by law to produce an annual report and accounts document. In addition to this, public companies commonly produce:

- *Quarterly and half-yearly results* Companies with shares quoted on the UK Stock Exchange are required to issue half-yearly statements. These are usually brief and contain the major financial highlights of the period.
- *Employee and shareholder reports* Many companies issue annual reports to employees and shareholders. As these, unlike the annual report and accounts, are not constrained by legal obligations in terms of form and content, they can give results in a more relevant and easily understood form.
- *A prospectus* When a company wishes to raise capital from the stock market it issues a prospectus. The prospectus contains information on the company's previous performance together with an assessment of its prospects. This type of document is not frequently published by a company because companies only rarely issue additional share capital.

In order to make full use of this chapter, you will find it useful to have a company annual reort to refer to. If you do not already have one available, you should normally be able to obtain one from the company secretary of any major company.

Please note that all major companies with shares issued to the public, are designated PLC or public limited company. Prior to 1980 all limited companies in the UK, whether they were quoted on the Stock Exchange or not, were called Ltd — limited. This name is now only applied to smaller companies without public shares.

22.2 What is the purpose of an annual report?

The main reason for producing an annual report is to satisfy the legal requirement to do so. The Companies Act lays down a set of minimum requirements for disclosure of information. They even describe the form in which it should be displayed.

The law requires that companies file their annual accounts with the Registrar of Companies. These laws have been enacted in order to protect third parties with an interest in the affairs of the company such as investors, creditors, employees and suppliers.

The legal requirement for financial reporting are supplemented by additional demands as laid down by the accounting profession and, for quoted companies, Stock Exchange regulations.

Much of the information supplied is therefore mandatory. Companies can, however, include additional information at their own discretion. The annual report presents the directors of the company with a good communication medium. Information can be included which satisfies shareholders and investors that optimum results are being achieved by the company and inspires confidence in the business. In other words, annual reports can, and often do, form a public relations exercise, although this latter information should not, of course, compromise the main aim of the report which is to provide a 'true and fair view of the state of affairs of the company' as required by the Companies Act.

The essential financial information provided must also be independently verified by suitably qualified accountants, that is, audited. The auditing process is an independent check on the stewardship of the company, as has been required from ancient times.

22.3 What the annual report contains

As mentioned previously, the contents of the annual report are defined by the Companies Act so that these reports have much more in common than we see in cost or management accounts. In addition, the controlling bodies of professional accountants lay down further rules of interpretation and practice for their members to follow. These are found in the *statements of standard accounting practice* (SSAPs) and other guidelines issued in the profession (some of the rules and conventions are shown below). Thus, both the accountants within the company, and the auditors, are charged with maintaining the agreed minimum contents and format.

The contents of the report can be broken down into a number of easily identifiable sections as shown below.

All reports will contain:

- the annual accounts statements and notes relating to them
- the directors' report
- the auditors' report.

Most reports will also contain the following:

- the chairman's statement
- a review of the company's activities
- a short summary of the company results
- a summary of the key results over the past five or ten years.

Exercise

If you have the annual report of your company available, locate the following items by recording the page numbers upon which they appear:

	Page
(1) The auditors' report	____
(2) The profit and loss account	____
(3) The notes on the accounts	____
(4) The directors' report	____
(5) Summary of results (if included)	____
(6) Five-year summary (if included)	____
(7) Source and application of funds	____
(8) The consolidated balance sheet	____

This should help you familiarize yourself with the contents.

You will find that the annual report and accounts of large businesses are often a summary of group activities and reflect the consolidation of the results of a large number of separate companies.

22.4 The rules and conventions observed by accountants

Companies' annual accounts statements form a significant part of the annual report. The directors of a company have the responsibility in law to ensure that the accounts reflect a 'true and fair view' of the affairs of the company. In other words, they must ensure that the published accounts reflect the real situation and are not misleading.

In practice, the responsibility for preparing the accounts is delegated to the accountants although the directors still have to take responsibility for the accounts by signing them.

The Companies Act contains most of the law by laying down the form and content of the annual report and accounts, but there are additional rules and conventions which must be observed by accountants. These rules and conventions are published by the accounting profession as guidelines designed to standardize the preparation process. As a consequence of these guidelines, interpretation and comparison of accounts is made easier for users. The principal rules and conventions are as follows:

- *Matching* The profit and loss account is prepared for a *period*, usually a year. The expenses to be charged against income or sales for that period are:
  - ★ those directly matching goods sold (not those involved in making unsold stocks)
  - ★ those incurred through the passage of time (depreciation, property rates, etc.).
- *Going concern concept* The values ascribed to the assets of the company should be on a 'going concern basis', assuming that the company will continue to operate in the foreseeable future. The reason for this is that different values might be ascribed to the assets if they had to be disposed of quickly, as in a company closure.
- *Consistency* Because there are many different assumptions and methods possible in the preparation of accounts, this convention insists that the accounts are prepared in a consistent manner, i.e. the same methods are used, from one period to the next.
- *Prudence* Again, because of the level of judgement necessary in the preparation of accounts (e.g. stock values, asset lives, bad debts, etc.), a prudent view should always be taken. So, for example, profits and assets should always be understated if there is any doubt as to their validity. Of course, this convention must be balanced against the need to produce a 'true and fair view'.
- *Materiality* This convention provides the common-sense rule that allows accountants and auditors to concentrate their efforts in the areas of greatest significance and value — known as 'material items'.

22.5 What the main sections of an annual report contain

Although both the minimum contents and form of presentation of the annual accounts are laid down in law, companies do have a certain amount of discretion over the order and appearance of the final document.

When reviewing the accounts of different companies, you should not necessarily expect to find the same item in an identical location within each report.

The directors' report
The directors of a public limited company are required by law (and by Stock Exchange rules) to provide certain information in the annual report and accounts. This requirement varies from general items such as the need to report on 'the state of the company's affairs', to specific items, for example, 'the amount of turnover arising from the export of goods'.

The accounting statements
The statements which companies are obliged to publish are: the profit and loss account, the balance sheet and the source and applications of funds statement. Some companies also include the value added statement. These statements are accompanied by a series of explanatory notes, forming part of the accounts.

The results portrayed are for the latest and previous accounting year (on occasions, such as when there is a change of accounting year date, a different time period may be used). For example, in the case of a company with a year ending on July 31st, the 1989 accounts will show profit and loss, and source and applications of funds, for both the year ended July 31st 1989, *and* that ended July 31st 1988. The balance sheet, the 'freeze-frame', is shown as it existed at those July 31st dates. This allows comparisons to be made on a time basis and indicates whether results are improving or deteriorating.

The notes to the accounts
The role of the notes to the accounts is to amplify the information given in the profit and loss and balance sheet statements. The notes must include a description of accounting policies and indicate the general accounting methods and assumptions used in preparing the accounts.

The remaining notes either amplify particular profit and loss and balance sheet lines, or convey general additional data. Most of the information supplied satisfies specific requirements of the Companies Act.

The additional data provided in the notes, but not specifically cross-referenced, principally concerns information that may interest third parties, such as:

- the payments made to directors

- commitments and possible future liabilities of the company. Commitments shown are capital projects which have been contracted and for which funds have been authorized but not so far spent. Contingent liabilities are sums of money that will be incurred by the company if certain events happen. Typical examples are loan guarantees, or possible penalties arising from current legal actions.

Notes on consolidated and company balance sheets

You may find that an annual report contains two balance sheets. Businesses are often operated as a group of companies and the *consolidated* balance sheet shows the combined results of the *group*. The second balance sheet contains the results of the *holding company* bearing the company title. In fact, an annual report will have been prepared for each of the UK limited companies. A legal requirement exists for each company to lodge accounts with the registrar of companies even if they are part of a group.

The auditors' report

All trading limited companies in the United Kingdom are required to have their accounts audited by a professional accountant. The Companies Act describe the minimum qualifications necessary for individuals to practise as auditors. They have to be either chartered or certified accountants.

The purpose of the auditor's report is to confirm to the people reading the report that the accounts presented give 'a true and fair view' of the affairs of the company. In other words, that the accounts have been prepared in accordance with the law and recommended accountancy practice. You may note that the audit report specifically restricts its comments to the accounts, and excludes items such as the directors' report.

Occasionally, auditors are not satisfied with the accounts of a company, and, if they do not reach agreement with the company, they issue what is known as a *qualified* audit report. In these cases, the auditors usually issue a statement to the effect that they agree the figures 'subject to' or 'except' the item(s) with which they are not satisfied.

At one time, qualifications were rare but nowadays, because some of the current accounting guidelines are controversial, company directors sometimes present accounts which are not strictly within the recommended guidelines, so that *technical* qualifications are quite common.

Fundamental qualifications arise in two major ways:

- The auditors feel that they are unable to verify that the accounts form a true and fair view because, for example, they do not have access to certain crucial information.
- They are able to form an opinion, but feel it conflicts with the accounts as stated. In other words they do not believe the accounts as stated represent a 'true and fair view'.

Because of the possible consequences of such a qualification — for example, a loss of public confidence in the directors — auditors must state their reservations in carefully couched terms. They must allow the person reading the report to draw correct conclusions without 'overstepping the mark'.

A fictional example of a qualified report is given below.

Auditors' report to the members of X Exports PLC

We have examined the accounts of X Exports PLC as set out on pages 10–20 in accordance with approved auditing standards.

As stated in note 15, some 50 per cent of the outstanding debtors figure, with a value of £1 million, relates to produce sold to the government of Y, which has subsequently been deposed. Continuation of the company's activities is dependent on the new government honouring this debt. Negotiations are currently in progress to secure payment of the amount outstanding.

The accounts have been drawn up on a going-concern basis which assumes that the debt will be collected, and no specific bad debt provision has been made.

Subject to a satisfactory outcome of these negotiations, in our opinion, the accounts, which have been prepared under the historical cost convention, give a true and fair view of the state of affairs of the company at 31st March 1989 and of the profit and source and applications of the company for the year then ended, and comply with the Companies Act 1986.

The qualification contained within this sample audit report reflects the reservations of the auditors regarding the value of the debtor asset shown.

22.6 Accounting policies

The accounting policies represent the rules under which accounts are constructed. As companies have grown in size and become more complex, the scope of the policies has increased. Many of them lay down approved valuation methods such as the basis of stock valuation, or depreciation rates. Others deal with more complex areas as, for example, the basis of consolidation and the treatment of foreign currency.

The basis of consolidation

In the simple accounts shown in the early chapters, the profit and loss statement and balance sheet were fairly easy to construct because we were dealing with a single company. For a group, in which the *consolidated accounts* contain the combined results of a large number of worldwide operations, the accounts are more complex.

The main factor making the accounts more complex is the fact that companies which are part of the group may not be wholly owned. In some cases, the group is not entitled to all of the company profits. The method used in consolidating the results of the individual companies depends therefore on the ownership. The categories, and the way in which the results are usually included, are as follows:

- *Wholly-owned subsidiaries* The individual company accounts of these companies are consolidated (added together) in a line-by-line way. In other words, each item in the profit and loss statement and balance sheet is added to the equivalent item in the accounts of the other companies to give group totals.
- *Subsidiaries in which the group owns the major controlling interest (50–99 per cent of shares)* These are consolidated in the same way as above, except that part of the profit and the capital is shown as belonging to *minority interests*. In other words, the minority shareholders are entitled to their share of the business and this is reflected by the accounts.
- *Related companies (less than 50 per cent of shares are owned)* In these, the group

is the minority shareholder, and the results are included in consolidation, only in so far as value of investment and earnings obtained. The group accounts only show the profit attributable to the group.

The rule here is generally intended to reflect managerial control. If you have control, it is proper to reflect full results, if not, only the profit proportion attributable is shown.

Accounting for currency

Another difficult area related to accounts consolidation is currency. International companies deal in foreign currency in two major ways:

- They have direct business transactions in foreign currency through sales to, and purchases from, overseas companies.
- Operations carried out through foreign subsidiaries, whose accounts are maintained in local currency, must be translated into sterling for the group results.

It is not our intention to go deeply into foreign currency translation other than to state that currency fluctuations can have a great effect on accounts as can inflation. The two effects are often combined, as in South America where some countries have inflation rates in excess of 100 per cent and wildly fluctuating exchange rates. It is easy, therefore, to produce unrealistic figures when results from these countries are expressed in sterling.

Accounting for taxation

Taxation is yet another complex accounting topic, the detail of which is outside the scope of this book — indeed most accountancy firms have specialists in this field!

It is worth mentioning, however, the major types of taxation with which a company has to deal:

- *Payroll taxes* A company is obliged to deduct PAYE and National Insurance payments from the wages and salaries of employees and pay these, together with employer's contributions, to the Inland Revenue.
- *VAT* A company has to account for value added tax on sales and purchases and acount for these to HM Customs and Excise.
- *Corporation tax* Companies have to pay tax at the corporation tax rate on net profits. The profit on which tax is paid is not the same as that shown in the accounts. This is because some costs are not allowed as tax deductible, the profit is therefore adjusted for non-allowable items.
- *Deferred tax* Under certain conditions, again mostly concerned with the timing of capital expenditure, the payment of taxation is deferred. At one time, most companies held large provisions for the payment of deferred taxation on their balance sheets. It has now been generally agreed that in most cases these payments will be deferred indefinitely, and the provisions consequently have been substantially reduced.
- *Advanced corporation tax* (ACT) When a company pays a dividend, it must pay ACT equivalent to the standard rate of income tax on the dividend payment. This ACT payment is, as its

name suggests, an advanced payment, which is, in most circumstances, deducted from the total corporation tax (the 'mainstream' tax) paid after the end of the financial year.

- *Capital gains tax* This is a tax on capital gains made on the sale of capital items. This tax applies to both individuals and companies.
- *Overseas taxation* Because the profits of overseas subsidiaries are usually taxed in the local country, it would be unduly harsh for them to be taxed again in the UK through the group accounts. For this reason the Inland Revenue allow double taxation relief by reducing the liability to UK taxation to mitigate the effects of double taxation.

CHAPTER 23

Analysing company accounts

This chapter lists the main users of company accounts and explains how basic analysis of company accounts may be initiated.

23.1 Who uses company accounts?

As the main formal vehicle for the publication of information about a company, the annual report has a varied audience outside the company. It is also a useful information base for internal management.

Each of the user groups requires different information. Because of this, the company may wish to provide an alternative publication to provide specific information to particular users. For example a *Chairman's Review* may be specifically aimed at the employee and shareholder groups.

The following groups are representative of most users:

- Private shareholders
- Professional investors, institutional shareholders, pension fund managers, Stock Exchange representatives
- Financial analysts and journalists
- Lenders of funds
- Business contacts — suppliers, customers, competitors
- Employees and their representatives
- Company management
- Governments and their agencies, such as taxation authorities, departments of trade and commerce, monopolies commissions, planners.
- The general public, such as local community workers, consumers, environmentalists.

The last two groups have extremely wide ranging needs which it is neither possible nor sensible wholly to satisfy at the same time as providing the mandatory business information required. Nevertheless, there is constant pressure on businesses to disclose more and more information.

23.2 How to start an initial analysis

You need to familiarize yourself with the general layout of a company report and accounts so that you can locate the various sections from which information for analysis can be abstracted. Results highlights are often provided, and for many casual users a quick look at these will be enough. However, proper interpretation requires further detailed investigation. In this section, a step-by-step approach is suggested. It will be most useful if you have a set of company accounts with you to refer to as you read through the rest of this chapter.

So, having familiarized yourself with the report contents, you can now analyse it.

Step 1: The auditors' report
The first step in analysing a set of accounts is to review the auditors' report. This will

tell you whether the accounts presented give an accurate reflection of business performance. In other words, it will indicate if there are any areas where we will have to exercise caution, or even give us danger signals! As a general rule, the shorter the auditors' report, the better.

Step 2: Check the statement of accounting policy

The next step is to review the statement of accounting policies. What you are checking for here is consistency. If there have been any fundamental changes in the way that the accounts have been prepared, there will be a problem in comparing successive year's results. Over the past few years now accounting guidelines and draft guidelines have been issued on a series of areas such as:

- Accounting for deferred taxation
- Accounting for foreign currency translation
- Group accounts.

Many of these have led to widespread changes in the methods by which results in these areas have been reported year by year. When a company changes an accounting policy it is obliged to disclose the fact and explain how it affects the accounts. In addition to this, the previous year's figure will also be adjusted, thereby enabling proper comparisons to be made.

The accounting policies used are also important when comparing a number of different sets of accounts as the policies used can affect the results significantly.

Step 3: Initial financial analysis

An initial financial analysis can be performed using the summarized results (the five- or ten-year record of results, if these are included).

What you should look for here are trends which only become apparent over a number of years. These should be obvious without any detailed analysis being necessary. The trends often become clearer if the key information is laid out in graphical form. The main areas to examine are revenue and profit growth, although you may also look at any other items you consider important.

In looking at these trends, you might also identify areas that would benefit from more detailed investigation in subsequent analysis.

Step 4: Taking the effects of inflation into account

Some companies now produce figures in their annual accounts which revalue their sales at current cost values. Obviously, in the case of groups with substantial overseas sales revenues this is extremely complex to achieve because not only do they have to take inflation in each country into account, but the movement of the source currency against sterling also has to be considered.

Nevertheless, we know that the costs of raw materials and labour do rise each year in most countries and sales revenue must therefore increase by an equivalent percentage in order for a company just to 'stand still', let alone grow. If the company does not provide inflation-adjusted figures, we can always make our own adjustments. With a UK company for example we can use an index such as the RPI (retail price index) in order to adjust the figures. You may remember that we identified a method of adjusting future figures to today's values, when we reviewed net present values in Chapter 20. We can do the same exercise

in reverse to present past figures at today's values for comparison.

To take an example, let us compare the actual sales figures achieved by a company over five years with the figures restated at current values. For the sake of simplicity we assume that the rate of inflation has been 10 per cent for each of the five years. Our sales restated line, shown below, represents the actual sales figure for each year multiplied by a factor to give the equivalent value as at year five.

Conversion to current year (year 5) values

Year	*1*	*2*	*3*	*4*	*5*
Actual sales (£m)	90.5	110.2	122.8	131.4	139.8
Sales restated (£m) (to Year 5 values)	132.5	146.7	148.6	144.6	139.8

So what looked like a sales growth pattern (from £90.5 million to £139.8) in the period, is actually only growth from £132.5 million to £139.8 million after inflation has been taken into account. Furthermore during years 4 and 5 sales, growth has not kept pace with inflation. This can be seen more clearly when the numbers are plotted on a graph as shown below:

Figure 21: 'Real' vs apparent sales growth

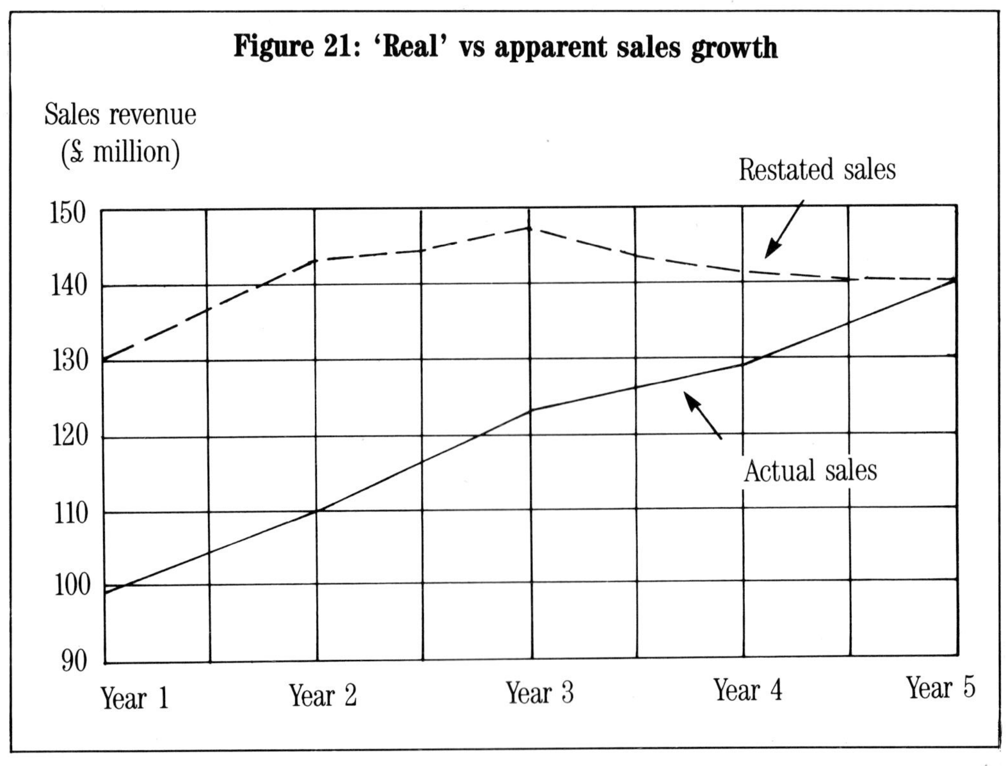

In the initial analysis you may well wish to consider other financial indicators in the summarized results, such as profit as a percentage of capital employed, or earnings per share.

As you have been going through the steps of this initial analysis you should also pick up a great deal of background information about the company being investigated and the environment within which it is operating. The areas to be covered include:

- General knowledge of the company
- The markets for the company's products or services, e.g.
  - ★ Is it dependent on one product or market?
  - ★ Does it operate in growing or declining markets?
  - ★ Is it investing in new products and markets?
- Its reputation and image:
  - ★ Does it have a good reputation for efficiency and innovation?
- Is it the leader in the industry? Who forms the major competition and how good are they?
- How active is the company in overseas markets? Are there good growth prospects overseas?
- Has the company diversified into new areas? How successful is this proving?
- How much is the company being affected by outside factors, such as inflation or recession?

This is obviously not an exhaustive list of areas to be considered, but it indicates the lines along which you should be thinking when assessing the state of a company. This general knowledge helps explain the financial analysis by providing answers for many of the numerical trends uncovered.

CHAPTER 24

The annual accounts statements

This chapter shows how company accounts may be analysed. The analysis is based on figures published by Lucas Industries PLC in their report and accounts for 1984.

The problem with annual accounts is the large volume of information available for analysis. In order to make sensible use of the figures, it is necessary to organize them in a logical and understandable way. Several techniques go beyond simple inspection, and provide a framework for this type of analysis such as 'common size' statements.

But first of all let us inspect the Lucas Industries profit and loss and balance sheet statements for 1983 and 1984 as they are presented. (We will only review the consolidated statements for the whole group.)

24.1 The profit and loss account

The first analysis of the profit and loss account should be by a simple year-on-year growth comparison:

	1984 £m	*1983* £m	*YOY growth* %
Turnover	1397.1	1216.8	14.8
Cost less other income	1331.2	1171.3	13.7
Trading profit	65.9	45.5	44.8
Other profits/(losses)	2.5	(0.8)	nil
	68.4	44.7	53.0
Net interest	20.5	24.6	(16.7)
Operating profit	47.9	20.1	138.3
Reorganization costs, etc.	15.3	18.0	(15.0)
Profit before tax	32.6	2.1	>1000
Taxation	14.3	12.3	16.3
Profit after tax	18.3	(10.2)	N/A
Other adjustments:			
Minority interests	1.4	2.6	
Extraordinary items	5.3	nil	
Dividends	8.2	8.2	
Transfer to/(from) reserves	3.4	(21.0)	N/A

So, what can now be concluded from this statement?

First of all, we must define some of the items:

- *Other profits/(losses)* represents Lucas Industries' share of profits/(losses) of related companies (those in which Lucas holds less than 50 per cent of shares). The revenues and costs of full subsidiaries are consolidated in the trading accounts above. In the case of related companies only the profit/(loss) to Lucas Industries is added in.
- *Minority interests* represents the profits of the company belonging to minority shareholders. Several Lucas subsidiaries have such shareholders. These minorities are not in a position to control the subsidiary company, but nevertheless are entitled to their share of profits or losses.
- *Extraordinary items* are items that derive from events or transactions outside the ordinary activities of the business which are both material and not expected to recur. Note 7 of the Lucas Industries accounts explains the detailed content in this case.

Some of the conclusions that may now be drawn are:

(1) The fact that revenue is now growing at a faster rate than costs is encouraging. As you can see even quite a small difference in rates (14.8 per cent growth against 13.7 per cent) on such large numbers can lead to a significant growth in trading profit (44.8 per cent).

(2) The interests in related companies are now showing a profit of £2.5 million compared with a £0.8 million loss in 1983.

(3) Net interest payments have fallen by 16.7 per cent.

(4) The amount being spent on reorganization, redundancy and closure is declining. Nevertheless, when the extraordinary item, which is also connected with closures of subsidiaries and disposals of investments in related companies, is taken into account, the figure is still high.

Overall, the company is showing significant improvements over the previous year, with a return to a positive transfer to reserves.

Further analysis of the profit and loss account may be performed using the notes. Thus sales and profit may be analysed by:

- Class of business (automotive, aerospace, industrial)
- Type of company (UK, overseas subsidiary, related company)
- Cost category etc.

Now do your own analysis by completing exercises 22 and 23.

Exercise 22

The following figures are taken from a note in the Lucas accounts. Calculate the percentage sales increase by geographical area and comment on the growth achieved by each in comparison with the overall growth of 14.8 per cent.

Area	*1984* *£m*	*1983* *£m*	*YOY growth* *%*
United Kingdom	665.0	585.7	
Rest of EEC	302.5	266.2	
Europe outside EEC	96.0	89.5	
North America	118.0	82.9	
Central and South America	39.8	31.8	
Australasia	49.6	50.0	
Asia	93.5	78.2	
Africa	32.7	32.5	
	1397.1	1216.8	14.8%

Exercise 23

The main categories of cost outlined in note 4 are outlined below again compare the item by item increases with the overall increase of 13.6% (for convenience the stock changes are included with raw materials and consumables).

Cost category	*1984* *£m*	*1983* *£m*	*YOY growth* *%*
Raw materials and components	494.6	423.0	
Staff costs	558.1	505.8	
Depreciation	36.6	30.9	
Other costs	250.3	219.6	
	1339.6	1179.3	13.6%

Common size statement

A common size statement is one in which all the figures are expressed in relation to a key figure. In this way, significant proportions and trends may be identified. In the case of the P&L, the obvious figure to use as a base is turnover. The common size P&L acount is shown below.

Common size profit and loss account

	1984		*1983*	
	£m	*%*	*£m*	*%*
Turnover	1397.1	100.0	1216.8	100.0
Cost less other income	1331.2	95.3	1171.3	96.3
Trading profit	65.9	4.7	45.5	3.7
Other profits/(losses)	2.5	0.2	(0.8)	nil
	68.4	4.9	44.7	3.7
Net interest	20.5	1.5	24.6	2.0
Operating profit	47.9	3.4	20.1	1.7
Reorganization costs, etc.	15.3	1.1	18.0	1.5
Profit before tax	32.6	2.3	2.1	0.2
Taxation	14.3	1.0	12.3	1.0
Profit after tax	18.3	1.3	(10.2)	(0.8)
Other adjustments				
Minority interests	1.4	0.1	2.6	0.2
Extraordinary items	5.3	0.4	nil	nil
Dividends	8.2	0.6	8.2	0.7
Transfer to/(from) reserves	3.4	0.2	(21.0)	(1.7)

The common size profit and loss statement presented in this way shows a number of different profit lines. The profit percentage definition used for 'return on sales' is profit before tax and interest. This is derived from the table by taking the profit before tax figure and adding the value for interest — which for 1984 is 2.3% + 1.5% = 3.8%.

24.2 The balance sheet

The Lucas Industries balance sheet presented in the vertical style

	1984 *£m*	*1983* *£m*	*Growth* *%*
Fixed assets			
Tangible assets	370.6	359.0	3.2
Investments	30.8	28.3	8.8
	401.4	387.3	3.6
Current assets and liabilities			
Stocks	309.2	291.1	6.2
Debtors	305.2	260.7	17.1
Cash at bank and in hand	28.2	23.9	18.0
	642.6	575.7	11.6
Creditors due within a year	(417.2)	(328.4)	27.0
Net current assets	225.4	247.3	(8.9)
Fixed and net current assets	626.8	634.6	(1.2)
Creditors due after one year	(108.9)	(132.1)	(17.6)
Provisions for liabilities and charges	(40.5)	(40.4)	0.2
	477.4	462.1	3.3
Capital and reserves			
Called up share capital	93.9	93.9	nil
Share premium account	24.4	24.4	nil
Profit and loss account	219.1	222.8	(1.7)
Other reserves	91.8	79.5	15.5
Shareholders' funds	429.1	420.6	2.0
Minority interests	48.3	41.5	16.4
	477.4	462.1	3.3

The sort of conclusions you might draw from this balance sheet might be as follows:

- The company is showing a small growth in total worth (3.3 per cent overall, 2.0 per cent attributable to Lucas shareholders).
- Investment in fixed assets is being held steady.
- Compared with the overall turnover growth of 14.8 per cent, an 8.9 per cent reduction in net working capital seems unusual. We will be interested to discover

whether this results from management control, or from other factors. The major elements of net working capital appear as follows:

- ★ Holding stock to 6.2 per cent growth shows good control.
- ★ The debtors figure consists of a number of different elements, the main one being trade debtors — money owed by customers against invoices. The growth in the trade debtors element of debtors is 14.8 per cent which is in line with sales growth.
- ★ There has also been a 60 per cent increase in prepayments — money paid by Lucas in advance — and accrued income — goods delivered but not yet invoiced.
- ★ The large growth in creditors needs investigating. The exercise below is designed to find the main cause.

Exercise 24

The rise in amounts due within one year could be due to either a lengthening of time taken to pay money owing, or to increases in the value of bank loans and overdrafts. The following figures have been abstracted from the relevant note. Which do you think is the principal cause?

	1984 *£m*	*1983* *£m*	*Growth* *%*
Amounts due within one year			
Trade creditors	166.5	134.2	
Payroll related creditors	42.6	40.4	
Accurals and deferred income	68.6	53.2	
Corporation tax and dividend	16.1	15.5	
Other	9.6	9.1	
Non-loan/overdraft creditors	303.4	252.4	
Bank loans and overdrafts (borrowings)	113.8	76.0	
	417.2	328.4	27.0

Now look at the common size balance sheet shown below. See how this statement further demonstrates trends. For example, the way in which debtors have moved from representing 56.4 per cent of assets in 1983, to 63.9 per cent in 1984 indicates a clear growth trend.

continued

Common size balance sheet

	1984 £m	1984 %	1983 £m	1983 %
Fixed assets				
Tangible assets	370.6	77.6	359.0	77.7
Investments	30.8	6.5	28.3	6.1
	401.4	84.1	387.3	83.8
Current assets and liabilities				
Stocks	309.2	64.8	291.1	63.0
Debtors	305.2	63.9	260.7	56.4
Cash at bank and in hand	28.2	5.9	23.9	5.2
	642.6	134.6	575.7	124.6
Creditors due within a year	(417.2)	(87.4)	(328.4)	(71.1)
Net current assets	225.4	47.2	247.3	53.5
Fixed and Net current assets	626.8	131.3	634.6	137.3
Creditors due after one year	(108.9)	(22.8)	(132.1)	(28.6)
Provisions for liabilities and charges	(40.5)	(8.5)	(40.4)	(8.7)
	477.4	100.0	462.1	100.0
Capital and reserves				
Called up share capital	93.9	19.7	93.9	20.3
Share premium account	24.4	5.1	24.4	5.3
Profit and loss account	219.0	45.9	222.8	48.2
Other reserves	91.8	19.2	79.5	17.2
Shareholders' funds	429.1	89.9	420.6	91.0
Minority interests	48.3	10.1	41.5	9.0
	477.4	100.0	462.1	100.0

24.3 The source and application of funds statement

Source and application of funds statement for Lucas Industries

		1984 £m		*1983* £m
Sources of funds				
Profit before tax		32.6		2.1
Depreciation (less profit from disposals)		35.3		29.6
		67.9		31.7
Less:				
Profit allocations (minority interests, related companies and extraordinary items)		9.4		0.1
		58.5		31.6
Proceeds from sale of fixed assets		10.9		12.3
Proceeds from sale of investments		3.2		1.0
Shares issued for assets or cash		6.1		22.6
		78.7		67.5
Application of funds				
Dividends paid		8.2		8.2
Taxation paid		14.3		12.6
Purchase of fixed assets		42.1		39.4
Increased working capital:				
Debtors	44.5		9.9	
Stocks	18.1		(17.2)	
Creditors	(53.0)		(17.0)	
Exchange adjustments	9.4		1.4	
		19.0		(22.9)
Investments and other		3.5		1.7
		87.1		39.0
Movement in net borrowings				
Balance at start of year	(177.5)		(206.0)	
Balance at end of year	(185.9)		(177.5)	
		(8.4)		28.5
		78.7		67.5

Conclusions that might be drawn from the source and application of funds statement:

- The generation of funds from trading has been far better in 1984 than 1983, as a result of the improved profit.
- In 1983 the funds were augmented by £22.6 million from shares issued in exchange for either cash or assets. However, in 1984 this was reduced to £6.1 million.
- With regard to funds applied to dividends, taxation and fixed assets, both years show a similar picture. However there is a marked difference in working capital funding between the two years. In 1983 debtors increased by a small amount; stocks were reduced, and creditors increased, which, after adjustment for exchange differences, caused a £22.9 million reduction in funds invested in working capital.
- In 1984, despite a very big increase in the creditor balance, the large increase in debtors led to an increased cash requirement of £19.0 million to fund working capital.
- By the end of the year an additional £8.4 million was needed to balance the cash books (generated by increased loans and overdrafts), compared with a £28.5 million reduction in borrowings during 1983.

This schedule shows the importance of maintaining good control of working capital when managing cash flows.

If you are wondering from where the borrowings totals have arisen (shown at the bottom of the statement), they are made up as follows:

From Note 14, Creditors:

	1984 *£m*	*1983* *£m*
Amounts due within one year		
Bank loans and overdrafts	(113.8)	(76.0)
Amounts due after more than a year		
Non-bank loans	(27.6)	(27.6)
Bank loans	(72.7)	(97.8)
Total borrowings	(214.1)	(201.4)
Less (from the balance sheet):		
Cash at bank and in hand	28.2	23.9
Net borrowings	(185.9)	(177.5)

Note
The credit values are shown in brackets.
There are many further types of analysis that can be carried out. For example, the ratios shown earlier in book are often applied. The type of analysis performed will need to be varied according to the information needs of the investigator.

Conclusion

This book was designed in order to provide a working knowledge of finance and accounts. It is only possible to provide a broad overview, given the scope and complexity of the subject. For further details of specific areas you will need to consult more specialized works. However, we hope that it has provided you with an insight into the main areas of the subject and that you will find what you have learnt of practical use.

Answers to exercises

Exercise 1: Your five factors should be based on the following list:

- Customer satisfaction
- Good profits
- Reinvestment in the business and markets
- Contented employees
- Efficient sales and production.

Exercise 2:

a) (c) — money owed by us
b) (d) — money owed to us
c) (c) — money owed by us
d) (d) — expenditure made
e) (c) — expenditure made
f) (c) — money owed by us
g) (c) — income.

Exercise 3: The answer should include the following:

Sources:
- From the owners — share capital.
- Borrowed — bank loans or mortgages.
- Reserves — money retained in the business.

Uses:
- Fixed assets.
- Current assets or working capital.
- Investments.

Exercise 4: The completed balance sheet should appear as follows:

Balance sheet of Light Manufacturing Ltd
31st December 198X

	£'000	*£'000*
Fixed assets		
Land and buildings	75	
Plant and machinery	**85**	
Office equipment	20	
Motor vehicles	30	

continued

	£'000	£'000
		210
Long-term investments		15
Current assets		
Stocks	**200**	
Debtors	120	
Cash	5	
	325	
Less: Current liabilities		
Creditors	(**120**)	
Bank overdraft	(20)	
	(140)	
Net current assets		185
Total net assets employed:		410
		£'000
Financed by:		
Owners' equity		
Share capital	200	
Reserves	**50**	
		250
Long-term loan		**160**
		410

Exercise 5(a):

Movements by balance sheet item during the year to 31/12/8Y

Item	*Balance 31/12/8X £'000*	*Net Movement £'000*	*Balance 31/12/8Y £'000*
Fixed assets			
Land and buildings	75	nil	75
Plant and machinery	85	+ 20	105
Office equipment	20	nil	20
Motor vehicles	30	+ 5	35
Investments	15	nil	15
Current assets and liabilities			
Stocks	200	– 20	180
Debtors	120	+ 30	150
Cash	5	nil	5

Item	*Balance 31/12/8X £'000*	*Net Movement £'000*	*Balance 31/12/8Y £'000*
Creditors	(120)	+(10)[more]	(130)
Bank overdraft	(20)	−(15)[less]	(5)
Share capital	200	nil	200
Reserves (Movement in year's profit)	50	+ 40	90
Long-term loan	160	nil	160

Balance sheet of Light Manufacturing Ltd as at 31st December 198Y

	198Y		*198X*	
	£'000	*£'000*	*£'000*	*£'000*
Fixed assets				
Land and buildings	75		75	
Plant and machinery	105		85	
Office equipment	20		20	
Motor vehicles	35		30	
		235		210
Long-term investments		*15*		*15*
Current assets				
Stocks	180		200	
Debtors	150		120	
Cash	5		5	
	335		325	
Less: Current liabilities				
Creditors	(130)		(120)	
Bank overdraft	(5)		(20)	
	(135)		(140)	
Net current assets		200		185
Total net assets employed:		450		410
Financed by:				
Owners' equity				
Share capital	200		200	
Reserves	90		50	
		290		250
Long-term loan		160		160
		450		410

Exercise 6(a):

Fixed asset category	*Cost 31/12/8X £'000*	*Additions during 198Y £'000*	*Cost 31/12/8Y £'000*
Land and buildings	75	nil	75
Plant and machinery	200	42	242
Office equipment	40	4	44
Motor vehicles	65	19	84
	380	65	445

6(b):

Fixed asset category	*Accumulated depreciation 31/12/8X £'000*	*Depreciation charged during 198Y £'000*	*Accumulated depreciation 31/12/8Y £'000*
Land and buildings	nil	nil	nil
Plant and machinery	115	22	137
Office equipment	20	4	24
Motor vehicles	35	14	49
	170	40	210

6(c):

Fixed asset category	*Cost at 31/12/8Y £'000*	*Accumulated depreciation 31/12/8Y £'000*	*Net book value 31/12/8Y £'000*
Land and buildings	75	nil	75
Plant and machinery	242	137	105
Office equipment	44	24	20
Motor vehicles	84	49	35
	445	210	235

Exercise 7:

		£'000
Working format:		
Sales turnover		500
Less: Cost of sales	250	
Other costs	160	
Trading profit		90

Light Manufacturing Ltd:
Profit and loss account for the year ended
31st December 198X

	£'000
Sales turnover	500
Trading profit	90
Income from investments	2
	92
Interest charges	17
Profit before taxation	75
Less: Taxation	35
Profit after taxation	40
Appropriation: Dividends paid	15
Retained profit	25

Exercise 8:

Light Manufacturing Ltd
Funds flow statement for the year ended
31st December 198X

		£'000
Sources of funds		
Profit before taxation		75
Add: Non-cash item depreciation		35
Funds from other sources: Sales of assets		10
Total funds generated		120
Uses of funds (applications)		
Capital expenditure		55
Dividends paid		15
Taxation paid		30
Working capital movements:		
(Increase/(decrease) in funds used)		
Increase in stocks	20	
Increase in debtors	10	
Increase in trade creditors	(5)	
Increased bank overdraft	(5)	
		20
Total funds used		120

Exercise 9: True or false? (Write T or F)

(a) Cost accounts, like annual financial report statements, have to be produced in a standard format. F

(b) Cost accounts unlike financial accounts use non-financial factors such as measurement of manpower hours. T

(c) Sometimes it is better to sacrifice 100% accuracy with cost accounts in order to produce timely reports. T

(d) Cost accounts are much more concerned with external reporting. F

(e) The presentation of financial accounts is largely determined by internal management needs. F

(f) When the financial and cost accounts derive from a common information base the system is known as an integrated system. T

(g) The role of cost accounts is to reflect the basic control factors in a business. T

(h) Auditors must validate the cost accounts system. F

(N.B. *Auditors are not* **compelled** *to, but they may well* **wish** *to validate the cost accounts as a measure of internal control.*)

Exercise 10:

- Marketing (Advertising manager) 8
- Manager of debt-collection 1
- Engineering support manager (responsible for production line maintenance) 2
- Sales manager 7
- Administration (customer enquiries) 3
- Personnel manager 6
- Flow-line production 5
- Work study engineer 4

Exercise 11:

Cost type	*Materials*	*Labour*	*Expenses*	*Cost code*
Bought-out components	X			1
Sales commission		X		5
Materials for research	X			8
Sheet metal for pressing	X			1
Press operator's bonus		X		2
TV advertisement			X	5
Production manager's salary		X		4
Advertisement for staff			X	7
Office cleaning services			X	7
Electricity for power press			X	3
Assembly workers' overtime		X		2
Fuel for delivery vans			X	6
Company rates bill			X	7
Engineering manager's salary		X		4
Machine repair parts	X			4
Office postage			X	7
Research scientist's salary		X		8
Salesman's car repairs			X	5

Exercise 12:

The simple answer is that some costs are much more easily managed and controlled than others. It is worthwhile therefore identifying those costs and paying most attention to them.

Exercise 13:

Step 1: Calculate overhead cost per unit.

	Cost centre 1	*Cost centre 2*
	£	£
Rent and rates (allocated by area £2,000 + £2,000)	2000	2000
Work study costs	5000	6000
Total overhead cost	7000	8000
Units produced	700	400
Overhead cost per unit (Total cost/units):	10	20

Step 2: Calculate total cost per unit.

	Cost centre 1	*Cost centre 2*
	£	£
Direct material cost	20	20
Direct labour cost	10	10
Overheads (from step 1)	10	20
Total cost per unit	40	50

Exercise 14:

(a) The factory manager's salary — F

(b) Component costs (constant per unit made) — V

(c) Quality checkers (1 per line up to 5,000 units produced, 2 over 5,000) — SV

(d) Electricity costs (£X per production unit throughput) — V

(e) Factory personnel department costs — F

(f) Plant maintenance costs (standard per 1,000 hours of operation) — V

(g) Royalty costs — the company pays a fixed fee of £100 for the first 500 produced, and then 5p per unit. — SV

Exercise 15:

Cash budget for Great Engineering Ltd

	£K	£K
Profit before tax (from P&L budget)		143
Add: Depreciation	34	
Proceeds from sale of fixed assets	10	
Proceeds from new capital	nil	
		44
Funds generated		187

Applications

Capital expenditure (from capital budget)	85
Investments purchased	nil
Taxation and dividend payments	64
Repayment of capital/loans	25

continued

	£K	£K
Increases/(decreases) in current assets		
(Increase)/decrease in liabilities:		
Stocks and WIP	nil	
Debtors	15	
Creditors	(10)	
		5
Cash surplus or (deficit)		8

Exercise 16:

						£m
Price variance	=	Unit price variance	×	Actual volume		
	=	£500	×	9,500	=	4.75m
Volume variance	=	Volume difference	×	Planned price		
	=	(500)	×	£4,500	=	(2.25m)
Total revenue variance (price less volume					=	£2.5m

Exercise 17:

	A	B
(a) Profit (Sales less costs)	£35,000	£27,000
(b) ROCE (profit/capital × 100)	14%	18%
(c) Net profit percentage (profit/sales × 100)	10%	4.5%
(d) Capital turnover (sales/capital)	1.4 times	4 times

Exercise 18:

Methods	*Description code (a–f)*
(1) Simple cash flow	c
(2) Discounted cash flow (DCF)	b
(3) Payback	f

continued

(4) Return on investment	e
(5) Internal rate of return (IRR)	a
(6) Net present value (NPV)	d

Exercise 19:

c = the ordering cost per unit = £20
d = annual rate of demand or usage = 12 × 1000 = 12,000
h = annual holding cost per unit = £3

Now use these numbers to complete the equation below:

$$\text{EOQ} = \sqrt{\frac{2cd}{h}} = \sqrt{\frac{2 \times 20 \times 12{,}000}{3}} = \underline{\underline{400}} \text{ tons}$$

Exercise 20:

Reasons why stock values should be kept *low* include:
(1) Costs of managing high stocks (premises, labour, insurance)
(2) High levels of stock wastage through deterioration
(3) Greater chance of wastage through obsolescence
(4) The cash tied up in stocks could be better used elsewhere

Reasons why stock levels should be kept *high* include:
(1) Bulk purchasing of raw materials
(2) Reserve or buffer stocks to smooth production
(3) The need to hold adequate finished goods stocks for customers
(4) Seasonal stock peaks
(5) Production efficiency 'making for stock'

Exercise 21:

$$\text{Average time to pay} = \frac{300\text{m} \times 12}{1400\text{m}} = \underline{2.57} \text{ months}$$

Note that a reduction in payment time of one week will release cash to the value of about £25 million.

Exercise 22:

Area	*1984*	*1983*	*YOY growth*
	£m	*£m*	*%*
United Kingdom	665.0	585.7	13.5
Rest of EEC	302.5	266.2	13.6
Europe outside EEC	96.0	89.5	7.3
North America	118.0	82.9	42.3
Central and South America	39.8	31.8	25.2
Australasia	49.6	50.0	(0.8)
Asia	93.5	78.2	19.6
Africa	32.7	32.5	0.6
	1397.1	1216.8	14.8

As you can see, Lucas has demonstrated good steady growth in the UK and EEC markets (some 70 per cent of total current business). Growth in the North American and Asian markets at 42% and 20% respectively was encouraging, as these represented the largest and fastest growing markets. The Australasian situation was commented upon in the Directors' Report, with the loss-making operations being halted.

Exercise 23:

Cost category	*1984*	*1983*	*YOY growth*
	£m	*£m*	*%*
Raw materials and components	494.6	423.0	16.9
Staff costs	558.1	505.8	10.3
Depreciation	36.6	30.9	18.4
Other costs	250.3	219.6	14.0
	1339.6	1179.3	13.6%

Comment:
Careful control of staff costs/increased productivity was the main factor contributing to higher profitability.

Exercise 24:

	198X £m	*198W* £m	*Growth* %
Amounts due within one year			
Trade creditors	166.5	134.2	24.1
Payroll related creditors	42.6	40.4	5.4
Accurals and deferred income	68.6	53.2	28.9
Corporation tax and dividend	16.1	15.5	3.9
Other	9.6	9.1	5.5
Non-loan/overdraft creditors	303.4	252.4	20.2
Bank loans and overdrafts (borrowings)	113.8	76.0	49.7
	417.2	328.4	27.0

Comment:
In this case the answer is that both total non-loan creditors and borrowings rose significantly (20.2 per cent and 49.7 per cent respectively). Trade creditors themselves rose by 24.1 per cent. Funding the business through slow payment is not popular with suppliers, and it would be interesting to know whether that is a deliberate policy, or merely a random payment fluctuation. The rise in borrowings payable within one year was offset by the decrease in borrowings repayable in over one year.

Index